Wicca Spell Book:

The Ultimate Wiccan Book On Magic And Witches

A Guide To Witchcraft, Wicca And Magic In The New Age With A Divinity Code

Julia Steyson

© 2018

COPYRIGHT

Wicca Spell Book: The Ultimate Wiccan Book On Magic And Witches A Guide To Witchcraft, Wicca And Magic In The New Age With A Divinity Code

By Julia Steyson

Copyright @2018 By Julia Steyson

All Rights Reserved.

The following eBook is reproduced below with the goal of providing information that is as accurate and as reliable as possible. Regardless, purchasing this eBook can be seen as consent to the fact that both the publisher and the author of this book are in no way experts on the topics discussed within, and that any recommendations or suggestions made herein are for entertainment purposes only. Professionals should be consulted as needed before undertaking any of the action endorsed herein.

This declaration is deemed fair and valid by both the American Bar Association and the Committee of Publishers Association and is legally binding throughout the United States.

Furthermore, the transmission, duplication or reproduction of any of the following work, including precise information, will be considered an illegal act, irrespective whether it is done electronically or in print. The legality extends to creating a secondary or tertiary copy of the work or a recorded copy and is only allowed with express written consent of the Publisher. All additional rights are reserved.

The information in the following pages is broadly considered to be a truthful and accurate account of facts, and as such any inattention, use or misuse of the information in question by the reader will render any resulting actions solely under their purview. There are no scenarios in which the publisher or the original author of this work can be in any fashion deemed liable for any hardship or damages that may befall them after undertaking information described herein.

Additionally, the information found on the following pages is intended for informational purposes only and should thus be considered, universal. As befitting its nature, the information presented is without assurance regarding its continued validity or interim quality. Trademarks that mentioned are done without written consent and can in no way be considered an endorsement from the trademark holder.

Table of Contents

Chapter 1: The Origins of Wicca 1
The Founding of Wicca 3
Later Developments 7
Shamanism 7
Paganism and Neo-Paganism 9
Magic 10
Is Wicca a religion? 11
Differing Traditions 13
Conclusion 15

Chapter 2: Wiccan Beliefs and Practices 16
The Wheel of the Year: Celebrating Sabbats 18
Esbats: Honoring the Moon 23
Astrology 28
Elemental Magic 32
Animism: The Soul of the World ...34
Tarot: Reading the Mirror 36
Conclusion 40

Chapter 3 Wiccan Deities and the Afterlife 42
Duotheism: The Horned God And The Triple Goddess 44
Polytheistic Practices 46
Hellenistic Wicca: The Pantheon of Olympus 47
Celtic Reconstructionist Wicca 50
Kemetic Pantheon 52

Norse Pantheon 55

Abrahamic Wicca 58

Conclusion 69

CHAPTER 4: WICCAN TOOLS 70

Altars and Altar Tools 70

Grimoires: A Witch's Diary 93

Herbs 96

Familiars Spirits: Animal Companionship 99

Other Wiccan Tools 101

Conclusion 102

CHAPTER 5: PRACTICING MAGIC 104

Magick and the Physical World 104

Moon Phases and Lunar Events 108

Chakras: Balancing Mind, Body, and Spirit 111

Spells 116

Sigils: The Conduits of Intention 119

Bath Magick 121

Conclusion 123

CHAPTER 6: FINDING YOUR NICHE 124

Choosing Your Path 125

Community Outreach 129

CONCLUSION 131

Chapter 1: The Origins of Wicca

Witches. Flying on broomsticks, wearing all black, huddled over cauldrons. Our pop culture idea of witches is full of images like that: green skin, a warted long nose. But as we grow older and wiser, we come to learn that witches are not as we have learned in our childhoods. While these tales may be good for entertainment, there is a rich spiritual history behind Witchcraft that is missed by these caricatures.

It is common and psychologically normal for people to fear what they don't understand. Our society has feared witches for centuries. Hundreds or even thousands of witches were killed in the Inquisition, witch hunts, and crusades. So much has been lost in the confusion that many people couldn't even begin to tell you what a witch is, or what witches believe and practice.

Today our society copes with the fear of that unknown by making a gentle mockery of a beautiful ancient tradition called Wicca. In this book, geared towards absolute beginners, we will hopefully shed some light on The Old Religion and its adherents.

The goal of this book is not only to educate, but to inspire. Even if you don't leave this book practicing Wicca, the hope is that you will find an understanding with those who do practice, and maybe also find a deeper appreciation for nature along the way.

However, this book serves not only as an educational guide for the curious, but can be used as an instructional how-to-begin for those who *are* interested in beginning their Wiccan journey. Simple explanations about holidays and beliefs are given, and the later chapters directly address how to begin the Wicca practice, while the early chapters are more for educational purposes.

There are more than a few rich traditions that fall under the umbrella of the term Wicca. In this chapter we will discuss the founding of Wicca, the influences on the religion, how Wicca is distinct from Paganism, and what the Wiccan ties are to magic. This chapter will also take a look at the different traditions of Wicca that have developed over time.

THE FOUNDING OF WICCA

Wicca is actually a modern religion, with fairly recent roots. However, it was not originally referred to as Wicca. The birth of what we now know as Wicca traces back to 19th century Britain, which was in the midst of an occult revival movement.

Gerald Brousseau Gardner (1884-1964) is often credited with founding in the 1920s what would expand into Wicca in the 1960s. Gardener studied the anthropological theory by Margaret Murray. This theory posited that an ancient pagan religion had been practiced during the rise and spread of Christianity in Europe. Murray called this religion a "witch cult" and postulated that those who practiced it did so in 13-person covens. Murray also wrote that they worshipped a "horned" god.

In the early 1940s, Gardener's extensive study of Murray's work as well as his deep interest in other authors who specialized in the Occult, inspired him to start his own coven. This was known by its members as the Bricket Wood coven.

In the beginning, around the 1920s-1950s before the term Wicca evolved with the New Age movement, they called it The Craft or The Old Religion. Gardner expanded the religion to include worship of a goddess and the Divine Feminine, along with elements of things he had learned from freemasons and ceremonial magic. We will discuss more about magic and its place in Wicca later in this chapter.

Gardner became friends with another early influencer of Wicca in 1947, Aleister Crowley (1875-1947). Crowley was known far and wide for his writings on the occult that were based on his personal experiences from participating in a wide range of esoteric religious traditions throughout his life. He travelled around the globe learning about Buddhism, Kabbalah (Jewish Mysticism), Astrology, Tarot, and Hindu practices as well.

Crowley is credited with being the first to distinguish magick with a "k" from magic. This was done so that there would be a specific word to differentiate his own religious practices from ceremonial magic, and stage magic that was popular during that time. Gardner adopted many rituals developed by Crowley.

However, nowadays Wiccans prefer to distance their practice from the influential Crowley because of his reputation as a misogynist and a racist. Discriminatory and bigoted perspectives are not considered to be compatible with the Wiccan way of life.

Crowley was also part of the reason Wiccan practices became publicly associated with Satanism. However, this connection is a false one; because Wicca is based on pre-Christian world views and concepts, Satan is not involved in any Wiccan ritual. In fact, Wiccan practice discourages any sort of "black magic" or association with evil.

This tradition is known today as Gardnerian Wicca. It brought many interested women occultists to his coven, including another influential person named Doreen Valiente (1922-1999). She became the High Priestess at Bricket Wood in the early 1950s. Valiente began a long period of religious revision in the material of the coven, in no small part to remove the association the coven had with Aleister Crowley.

Valiente felt that Crowley had made a mistake trying to mass market Witchcraft. Crowley was also known for silencing women who disagreed with them, limiting their participation in his rituals and in the Bricket Coven.

In 1957, Valiente began her own coven. She wrote several books and learned alongside many prominent occultist figures of the New Age religious movement. Valiente emphasized individualism in practice, and is a large reason the practice of Wiccans today is so diverse and varies so much between individuals and covens. Valiente really was the one who took Wicca from being a secretive practice done behind closed doors to a widespread phenomenon that many people suddenly had access to because of her work.

In the 1970s, Wiccan traditions finally made it out of England thanks to some other key influencers, who brought the Craft to the entire UK, the United States, and Australia. Because of this branching out, many different traditions formed. These traditions include those such as the Dianic, the Celtic, and the Georgian.

Alex Sanders (1926-1988) later founded what is now known as Alexandrian Wicca, which follows a specific set of traditions. Another sect was founded by Raymond Buckland in the 1970s, known as the Seax-Wicca tradition. Buckland wrote dozens of books on The Craft and is known as the person who brought Gardnerian Wicca to the United States.

Later Developments

Around the 1980s, Wicca had an estimated 50,000 self-proclaimed Wiccans that in some way practiced in the Northern Americas and western Europe. That growth slowed down significantly by the end of the century, but Wicca gained a considerable amount of social acceptance in that time. Wicca also continued to develop, with new rituals and practices being created by new Wiccans with every passing generation that upheld the Craft.

The Dianic Wiccans saw Wicca as a woman's religion, and the Neo-Pagan movement began to gain speed alongside Wicca. Neo-Paganism and Wicca are now represented to the world through two international organizations, the Universal Federation of Pagans and the Pagan Federation.

Shamanism

Many Wiccan practices are based in the concept of shamanism. *Shamanism* is an umbrella term for a lot of different practices. It began as an Eastern practice of advanced uses of herbal medicine. Shamans were highly revered in their societies for their medical skills and their ability to communicate directly with the spirit world. A shaman was often identified by having some kind of physical defect, seen as a trade for their special abilities.

Classical shamanism in Northern Asia believed that a shaman was aided by a spirit or even a group of spirits that helped them to heal and to define the future. Shamans could also connect with guardian spirits, who might be otherworldly or a lifetime partner in the mortal plane.

Shamans channeled the spirit world using sound and music, utilizing tools such as rattles, drums, and improvised songs to conduct their practice. This would most often be done by entering a trance state of consciousness.

Modern Wiccans no longer use the word Shaman, but instead have switched to the term "hedge witch". This will be explained in more detail in Chapter 6. Modern hedge witches channel the spirit world through trance, astral projection, and lucid dreaming.

PAGANISM AND NEO-PAGANISM

The term *Paganism* has long been used as a derogatory word for all non-Christian (primarily polytheistic) religions. For a long time the word served the same purpose as calling someone a heathen. However, in the modern day, Pagans and Neo-Pagans are reclaiming the title and the faith. While Wicca is considered a Pagan religion and is represented internationally by Pagan Federations, there are distinctions to be drawn between those who identify as Wiccans and those who identify as Neo-Pagans.

Pagan is used today as another umbrella term. According to the Pagan Federation International, "Pagans may be trained in particular traditions or they may follow their own inspiration. Paganism is not dogmatic. Pagans pursue their own vision of the Divine as a direct and personal experience."

One can see that Wicca easily fits within this definition of Pagan. There are traditions that can be chosen and adhered to within Wicca, but this is not a necessity to be a Wiccan (thus it is not a dogmatic religion). Wiccans also have a personal relationship with the Divine and their individual practices.

So what is a Neo-Pagan, and how are Neo-Pagans different from Wiccans? The answer may depend on who you ask.

Because the definition of Pagan is so intentionally vague, it can be hard to draw lines deciding where one tradition begins and where another ends.

According to Joanne Pearson, an occult writer, Wicca is both at the center of and on the margins of Neo-Paganism. The former is stated because the history of Wiccanism and Neo-Paganism has a very large amount of overlap; at the core, they were both born out of the 19th century Occult movement and popularized through the New Age Movement in the 1960s and 1970s.

Magic

In what way is Wicca inherently tied to magic? Some Wiccans would offer that Wicca is in no way inherently related to magic! This is because some Wiccans don't include any magic elements in their practices. That's right -- you can be Wiccan without practicing magic! Many Wiccan rituals are focused around revering nature and don't focus on supernatural elements.

That being said, there are many whom their Wiccan practices are inseparable from magic practices. There are, as was mentioned much earlier in the chapter, distinctions to be drawn between different types of magic.

Ceremonial magic, also known as High Magic, predates almost anything else that Wiccans and Pagans draw from. This kind of magic is known for being elaborate in its ritual. Sometimes this magic is done to appease a God by collecting a variety of different things that would please that deity and using them in a specific manner and order. For this reason, ceremonial magic is also known as ritual magic; the two terms are often used interchangeably.

Practical magic is magic that is used in one's day to day life. Sigils, simple spells, enchantments...the purpose of this kind of magic is to make a small, but direct change to everyday life by channeling your own personal magic. This is what is sometimes referred to as magick. This book will use the "k" spelling to distinguish that this is the type of magic being discussed.

Is Wicca a religion?

This question is a deceptively difficult one to answer. First of all, it depends on how one defines religion. Many definitions of what 'religion' is have been specifically written to exclude nature-based religions, including Wicca and First Nations religions. Some consider this to be a form of supremacy, while other Wiccans would rather be distanced from organized religion in the first place.

Whether or not Wicca is considered a religion by the world at large, is it considered to be a religion by adherents of Wicca? While some would say yes, I think it's important to consider the voices of Wiccans who would say no. Some Wiccans consider Wicca to be a practice rather than a religion.

This is partially because most organized religions are composed of Orthodoxy and Orthopraxy. Orthodoxy is when one holds "correct" beliefs and is generally considered by Wiccans to be dogmatic and against Wiccan values. Orthopraxy is "correct" practice, which while important to Wiccans, there is no supreme doctrine to determine what the correct way to practice Wicca is.

Some Wiccans that adhere to a specific tradition may value orthopraxy, but no Wiccan would ever tell another Wiccan how to practice authoritatively. Instruction is given through a loving intention, not because there is a right or wrong way to do something.

Some Wiccans don't identify Wicca as a religion because they believe it is a specific decision *against* religion. Others consider it to be a universal religion. Like many things in Wicca, there is no definitive, dogmatic yes or no answer.

Differing Traditions

As you've seen by now, there are many different traditions that have developed over the course of the history of Wicca. This is undoubtedly because of the influence of Doreen Valiente, who emphasized the importance of individualistic practices and beliefs in her influential books during the rise of early Wicca.

In this subsection we will discuss just a few of the main traditions of Wicca, although many Wiccans consider themselves to practice outside of the guidelines of these traditions. Even a Wiccan living outside a tradition may pull rituals from traditions that speak to them.

Gardnerian Wicca focuses on recreating the original teachings and rituals of Gerald Brousseau Gardner himself. Gardner painstakingly recreated rituals he had extensively researched, and wanted to challenge mainstream religion. For example, many of the rituals are performed without any clothes on, to become closer to the natural state. Rituals are focused on nature and involve a creative, bright use of color to represent elements and energies. However, this tradition is also very rule-based, and many have found it to be somewhat constricting.

Alexandrian Wicca was founded by Alex Sanders, who was the self-proclaimed "King" of the witches in his coven. Alexandrian Wicca can seem very similar to Gardnerian, mimicking their naked rituals and coven rites, but has more ancient Jewish influences from Kabbalah.

Georgian Wicca was founded by George Patterson in California in the 1970s. While Georgian Wiccans follow the general example of Gardnerian Wicca and Alexandrian Wicca, the coven is much more flexible and individualistic. Coven members sometimes make up their own rituals. Patterson used to say regarding rituals, "If it works, use it. If it doesn't, don't."

Dianic Wiccan, named after the Greek Goddess Diana, was founded by Zsuzsanna Budapest. Since its inception in 1970s, Dianic Wicca has been known as a particularly feminist branch of the Craft. Only goddess figures are worshipped, and many covens only accept women. Dianic Wiccans are also known for their political activism.

Eclectic Wicca is a fast-growing tradition that believes that no formal tradition or doctrine is necessary for one to be a true Wiccan. Eclectic Wiccans ignore institutions that are in place such as initiation, secrecy, and the hierarchical structures of covens.

Conclusion

We've now gotten a taste for the beginnings of what we today know as Wicca. We've discussed history and related terms, and traditions that Wicca has pulled from to become the complete, independent religion (or religion alternative) it is today.

But if one can truly be a Wiccan without subscribing to a tradition, then what exactly is it that makes someone a Wiccan? Well, although beliefs vary widely from Wiccan to Wiccan, there are some core beliefs that most Wiccans hold. These will be discussed in the coming chapter.

Chapter 2: Wiccan Beliefs and Practices

Modern Wiccans hold a wide range of beliefs and practice is very individualistic, making it hard to define Wiccan beliefs in an exact way. There are, however, some more common, core beliefs that most Wiccans ascribe to. For example, this chapter will discuss that many Wiccans engage with elemental magic, Tarot, and celebrate the festivals of The Wheel of the Year. Esbats and Animism will also be discussed in this chapter to gain a well-rounded grasp on general Wiccan ideals and practices.

The core of Wiccan beliefs teaches us that our practice is our own as long as we are doing no harm to others. Unless you have taken the role of a High Priestess or a Coven Mother, or some other teaching role, it is discouraged to instruct others on how to perform their Craft. Of course offering helpful tips is no problem, but imposing your rules on someone else is against the Wiccan way of life.

All Wiccans, whether they practice magic or not, have a worldview focused on reverence for nature. The Divine lies all around us in the spirits that inhabit us and the natural world. Everything is connected, and a Wiccan treads lightly to maintain the harmonious balance of the Mother Earth.

All Wiccans also worship feminine aspects of the divine alongside their masculine counterparts. In order for there to be balance in the universe, there must be balance among masculine and feminine spirituality and worship.

THE WHEEL OF THE YEAR: CELEBRATING SABBATS

The Wheel of the Year is the name given to the cycle of festivals held annually by Wiccans and also some Neo-Pagans. Wiccans celebrate all eight festivals of the Wheel of the Year. The solstices and equinoxes make up four of the eight holidays and are known as the quarter days or cross-quarter days. They are the midpoint festivals of the year, celebrating the seasons.

A *solistice* is a celestial event, where the Sun is positioned in its most Northerly or Southerly quadrant in its travel relative to the equator of the Earth. There are two solstice events a year. While the names for festivals vary widely between different Wiccan traditions, the names commonly used for the solstice celebrations are the Midwinter Yule festival and the Midsummer Litha festival.

The *Yule* festival has been celebrated since the late Stone Age. It is known as the turning point of the year, and for many is the most important festival to honor in the entire year. The Sun is an important symbol during this festival, its ebbing in the sky during sunset often seen as a symbol of renewal, fertility, and rebirth.

The Yule festival is celebrated in many various ways, depending on the person, the coven, and the Wiccan tradition being emulated. Common celebrations include making sacrifices, feasting, and giving gifts to those you care about are common elements. Decorations include evergreen plants such as pine and seasonal winter plants such as holly. Tree decorating is also a Wiccan practice at this time, similar to current western Christian traditions for Christmas

The *Litha* festival is one of four solar events being celebrated as a solstice event. This summer festival celebrates the sun shining for the longest of any day of the year. Bede writes that "Litha means *gentle* or *navigable*, because in both these months the calm breezes are gentle and they make one want to sail upon the smooth sea."

The Litha festival is typically celebrated by going outside and reconnecting with nature while the sun is shining. Hikes and drum circles are common celebratory events held. Prayers are said to honor the season, and this is also known as a time of learning and charity within the Wiccan community.

An *equinox* is another celestial event, when the center of the Sun crosses over the equator of the Earth. This occurs twice a year. The equinox festivals are known as the Ostara festival for the Vernal Equinox, and the Mabon festival for the Autumnal equinox.

Ostara is the Spring equinox celebration, during which day and night stand exactly equal in time, with light on the increase. Some celebrate on the day of the equinox, while others celebrate Ostara on the full moon after the equinox because of the festival's association with the feminine and the Goddess Aphrodite.

During Ostara Wiccans eat traditional vegetable and herb based dishes, using whatever spring ingredients are native to their area. Floral incense is used, traditionally jasmine or rose. Daffodils and Violets are fresh flowers that are often used in Ostara rituals to promote prosperity in the time of coming light, sometimes in combination with the stone Jasper.

The festival *Mabon* is also known as the Harvest Home, and the Ingathering Feast. Mabon is celebrated in the autumn and is a time to give thanks to the universe, nature, and deities for the annual gifts we have received. Like Ostara, the day is divided equally into night and day, but this time we are paying respects to the coming days of darkness.

Mabon is celebrated by making offerings in thanks for the gifts nature and the Gods and Goddesses have given us. In the Druid tradition, offerings are made to celebrate the fruit-giving trees. Offerings most often include ciders and wines, along with autumn herbs. This celebration is one of the most lavish occasions, and Wiccans often wear their best finery.

The secondary holidays are often cause for large celebrations as well, despite being less important celestial events. These holidays are generally called Imbolc, Beltane, Lammas, and Samhain.

Imbolc usually occurs on the first day of February and is a celebration of the first inklings of spring beginning to sprout through the winter frost. Historically a Celtic holiday, for Wiccans this is a time to purify oneself and one's tools, and to do spring cleaning. Dianic Wiccans have coven initiations during this time, and for all Wiccans it is representative of renewal of faith and dedication to the Craft.

Traditionally on the first day of summer in Ireland, *Beltane* also has Celtic roots. Beltane was traditionally to celebrate Flora, the Goddess of flowers. Dancing around a lively bonfire is the most common way Wiccans celebrate this time of season. In duotheistic Wiccan lore, this is the time when the Horned God and the Triple Goddess are perfectly united.

Lammas is celebrated on the first day of August and is another Harvest festival. This holy day is to celebrate living off the land, to celebrate grains in particular in the early beginnings of fall. It is common to weave dolls out of grain husks such as corn husks to honor the Gods and Goddesses of the harvest.

Commonly celebrated by non-Wiccans as Halloween, *Samhain* is often a favorite celebration of Wiccans everywhere. Opposite the yearly calendar to Beltane, Samhain is a holiday to honor those who have passed into the great beyond. Ancestors, elders, friends, and even pet familiars are honored at this time. It is a holiday to show love to all those that have passed who have supported us, and those who continue to support us each day.

Samhain is typically celebrated by connecting with the spirit world in some ritual way, because Wiccans believe this is the time of the year that the veil between the natural and the supernatural is the thinnest. Samhain is also spent lighting candle vigils for those we choose to honor and remember on this Day of the Dead.

ESBATS: HONORING THE MOON

An *Esbat* festival is a festival which is intended to show honor and respect for the moon and Her influence on the natural world. It is a time in which the coven gathers besides the main Wheel of the Year celebrations or the Sabbat. Janet Farrar, a known occultist writer, describes esbats as an opportunity for a "love feast, healing work, psychic training and all."

Esbats occur on a full moon. Some covens that focus on the moon in particular extend these practices to dark moons, and to the first and last quarters of the moons during the month. While the main festivals are times for celebration, the important magickal work of the year is completed during the Esbats.

An Esbat traditionally begins at midnight and finishes at the break of dawn, called cock-crow by many traditional Wiccans for this ritual. Esbats are a complete celebration of the feminine, and the full moon represents Mother Earth impregnated with spiritual energy. Dancing, singing, and magickal rituals are common at Esbats. If one is not part of a coven, often this is done amongst other Wiccan friends.

If the Esbat is done during a full moon, this considered to be one of the most powerful times to perform magick. Crystals and stones are charged with the raw healing and purifying energy of the full moon. Other things, such as water and Tarot decks may be charged with this energy as well, along with a large list of other magick tools.

During a dark moon, however, Wiccans abstain from magick practices. Instead, the focus is turned on inner demons. Meditation and trance states are common ways that dark moons are honored. The goal during a dark moon is to address and conquer the darkness which exists inside all of us.

The waxing of the moon, when the moon is growing larger, is a good time for "positive" spells -- spells that help you gain things like love and wealth. The waning of the moon is a good time for "negative" spells -- spells that help you lose bad habits, or leave something spiritually blocking behind.

The Moons of different months have different names that go along with their different energies. These different energies are important to be aware of, as they may make particular times of year perfect for certain magickal goal.

The January Moon is known as The Wolf Moon or The Winter Moon. Seen as a time to remember things that are coming to an end and also a time to look forward to new beginnings, this moon represents protection and strength.

The February Moon is also known as The Storm Moon or The Death Moon. In centuries past, the brutal cold of this month made it a time of hardship for those practicing the Old Religion who lived off the land. This is a time for spells focused on fertility for the coming Spring.

The March Moon is often called The Chaste Moon or The Seed Moon. This is a time to plant "seeds" in your mind. You press ideas of imagination, creativity, and prosperity, and speak them into existence with chants, spells, and songs. This month of purity and newness is the perfect time to prepare yourself for the coming flora of Spring.

The April Moon is also known as The Egg Moon or The Grass Moon. If you keep a magickal garden, this is the perfect time to begin planting under the Esbat moons. While in March we sowed seeds of the mind, now we sow literal seeds into the Earth. April is a time for action.

The May Moon is sometimes called The Hare Moon or The Flower Moon. This opens the gates of love and romance. This is a good time for love spells and to focus on your romantic partner(s). Rekindling the spark in a relationship is never more possible than during a May Esbat ceremony.

The June Moon is The Lovers Moon or The Rose Moon. This passionate time is perfect for spiritually encouraging romantic engagements and marriages. This is also a time for those who are single to engage in spiritual prosperity spells.

The July Moon, also known as The Mead Moon or The Lightning Moon, is a time of health and enchantment. Mead is the nectar of the Gods, and the time for prosperity and strength is on the rise now powered by the heated energy reflected from the Summer sun.

The August Moon is called The Red Moon. This occurs during Harvest time, a time of abundance. This is another month where marriage magick is strong, and where the fruits of the prosperous summer are given thanks for.

The September Moon is also known as The Harvest Moon. Following August this is another month of abundance during which thanks are given for the fruits of the Autumnal harvests. The Harvest Moon can help bring you and those you care about much prosperity, which you may need in the harsher months to come.

The October Moon is often called The Blood Moon. This is a time of renewal of faith and dedication to the Craft. This is a great time to set new goals for the coming Winter season. Divination is also fueled by extra spiritual energy during October Esbats, so the time for Astrological and Tarot readings is nigh.

The November Moon, sometimes known as The Snow Moon, acknowledges the passing of the abundance of the past seasons. This is a time to connect spiritually with those who mean the most to you, whether they're family, friends, coven members, or your community at large. Emotional bonds can be made stronger through rituals during The Snow Moon Esbats.

The December Moon is also known as The Oak Moon or The Cold Moon. Because the nights have become longest at this time of the year, this is a time to reflect on the true power of the moon. The Moon has dominion over the spirit world during December because the nights are longer than the days. The thoughts of Wiccans turn again towards rebirth and the promise that Spring will return again. Let go of the negative and let the light of the day live on through your spirit during this dark time of year.

ASTROLOGY

You've probably heard of astrology at one point in your life, and might even know your astrological Sun Sign (sometimes called a Zodiac Sign), because it's based on your birthday - Sagittarius, Capricorn, or what have you.

For centuries people have been using the celestial bodies to predict mundane, worldly events in our lives. Many Wiccans also believe that the stars have a large amount of influence over world events and human emotions. *Astrology* is a type of divination that focuses on interpreting patterns in the planets, Moon, and stars in order to foresee earthly events.

Only since our modern era of scientific revolution took hold did Astrology become discredited as an actual science itself. Thus, it is no surprise that there is much research and nuance behind it that can make astrology seem intimidating and complicated. However, the rich balance between rules and intuition are part of what makes Astrology so effective and attractive to some Wiccans.

Astrology draws on Hellenistic philosophy as well as the model of physics introduced to the world by Aristotle. This means that Astrology regards the movement of the celestial bodies as eternal, while the motions of the four elements (Fire, Earth, Air, and Water) are linear.

Astrology has never been intended to be an exact science, because no one person can truly, completely understand the order of the cosmos. This is also because while Astrology is made to predict trends in human mood and behavior based on the effect of the stars, having divined these things, humans are capable of changing the outcomes despite the influence of the celestial bodies. Divine intervention is another possibility.

Most of us know our Sun Sign, which is the principle sign that forms our personality according to Astrology. There are 12 houses in each person's natal charts, based on where each planet, Moon, or star was when that person was born.

These 12 houses interact with one another to create your full, incredibly nuanced personality. Your Moon Sign, for example, affects the manifestation of your Sun Sign. An emotionally-in-touch Cancer might gain vanity and confidence from having their Moon Sign positioned in Leo, for example. Other planets control other domains in your life. Venus reigns over one's love life, and the Midheaven sign gives us insight into our life's work.

Each astrological sign is related to a planet, an element, and also has a special relationship with either male or female energy. The chart below is a handy way to check out which ones align with your sign!

Sign	Date	Nature	Element	Planet	Symbol
Aries	March 20 – April 20	Masculine	Fire	Mars	Ram
Taurus	April 20 – May 21	Feminine	Earth	Venus	Bull
Gemini	May 21 – June 21	Masculine	Air	Mercury	Twins
Cancer	June 21 – July 2	Feminine	Water	Moon	Crab

Leo	July 22 - August 23	Masculine	Fire	Sun	Lion
Virgo	August 23 - September 23	Feminine	Earth	Mercury	Maiden
Libra	September 23 - October 23	Masculine	Air	Venus	Scales
Scorpio	October 23 - November 22	Feminine	Water	Mars	Scorpion
Sagittarius	November 22 - December 21	Masculine	Fire	Jupiter	Archer

Capricorn	December 21 - January 20	Feminine	Earth	Saturn	Sea-Goat
Aquarius	January 20 - February 18	Masculine	Air	Saturn	Water-Bearer
Pisces	February 18 - March 20	Feminine	Water	Jupiter	Fish

ELEMENTAL MAGIC

The natural elements that are involved here have a large place in the world of Wicca and magic. Similar to how the placement of the stars can affect outcomes, we can predict the behavior of certain things based on their association with the elements. For example, crystals and gemstones that are associated with water are more likely to be used for healing.

While most people know of the four classical elements, Wicca believes in a fifth element that begins where the other four connect. This element is called Aether, meaning spirit. Use of the elements helps keep our practice directly in line with nature. The elements can metaphorically represent emotional and spiritual characteristics as well as the literal connection to nature.

Air dominates the aspect of magic that revolves around visualization. Air is a masculine element that is associated with the Eastern direction. Air represents intelligence and mental faculties, psychic abilities, imagination, ideas, the mind, dreams, and inspiration. Associated with the spring, some symbols of Air include the wind, the sky, the breeze, feathers, breath, clouds, herbs, and some flowers. Wind instruments such as the flute may be used to channel Air energy.

Fire is representative of magick itself. Fire is a masculine element that is associated with the Southern direction. Fire represents change and is the most physical and spiritual of all the elements. Ruled by passion, fire is often invoked through symbols such as candles, incense, baking, love spells, and burning objects.

Water represents cleansing and healing, and is a feminine element associated with the Western direction. Water is a receptive energy. Water itself can be easily enchanted and charged and holds energy from its surroundings very easily. Water is a dynamic representation of the subconscious emotional world, the soul, and wisdom.

Earth represents strength and is a feminine element associated with the Northern direction. Earth is manifested in abundance, wealth, prosperity. Rituals invoking the Earth element often involve burying an object to infuse it with strong energy promoting good fortune in finance.

Aether is a universal element representative of the spirit world and individual spiritual entities. Aether is the element present in some form in all things (see Animism later in this chapter). Associated with The Horned God and The Triple Goddess, Aether connects all natural things and allows the world to exist in a careful harmonious balance.

ANIMISM: THE SOUL OF THE WORLD

Animism is a religious belief system that holds the value that everything on earth, including inanimate natural objects, has a soul or a distinct spiritual essence. The title comes from the

Latin *anima* which means "spirit", "breath", and "life". Animism perceives all natural things to be "alive" in the sense of having Aether, the spirit of the universe within.

It is the belief that all things of nature, sticks, rocks, animals (including humans), clouds, the wind, all these things are interconnected. The world feels the effect of the loss of any natural thing, and the balance must be maintained.

Animism was originally an ancient Indigenous belief -- that is, it was held by a large number of First Nations and Native American tribes. Wiccans often intermingle practices with First Nations religious practices because of their shared respect for the natural world. Animism is recognized as the oldest known world religion, although of course it was not an organized religion as we know today.

Those who believe in Animism today are almost always religiously pacifist, refusing to harm or kill any other being or object that contains spirit. In this way we preserve the balance, respect our place in nature, and learn to live in harmony with our environment.

Those who do not practice pacifism may choose to engage with this balance directly by hunting and gathering. Living off the land is a different approach that puts one in the middle of that balance. It teaches one how to maintain that harmony while facing the reality that, as humans, we must consume natural things to maintain our own lives.

Whether a hunter, gatherer, omnivore, or vegan, all Animists choose to honor that which they take from nature in some say. It could be in the form of a ritual, perhaps honoring the kills of the hunt before consumption or having special sacrificial rites to honor the spirits.

Nature is also honored during every Wiccan festival, but Harvest festivals in particular aim to acknowledge and give thanks for the natural blessings we receive that allow us to continue to exist.

Tarot: Reading the Mirror

Many entire books could be and have been written about the subject of divination via Tarot. Tarot cards first began being used in recorded history for divination purposes in the 18th century in European countries like France and Italy.

However, many occult authors trace the unwritten history of Tarot back to ancient Egypt or ancient Kabbalah practices.

There are many different styles of Tarot readings, including those from French, Celtic, and Kabbalistic backgrounds

Tarot isn't meant to be a tool to exactly read the future, either. Tarot is simply a way to measure the forces at work on the current circumstances. The outcome is in control of the seeker. The goal of Tarot is to guide the seeker and advise them of the cosmic energies at work. .

In fact, the best way to think about Tarot is a reflection of the self. The cards contain imagery that has been meaningful to humankind for centuries, and which are ingrained in what psychologist Carl Jung would call our unconscious. The cards tell a story about cosmic forces, but the cards also help us learn about ourselves in how we understand the stories the cards tell.

Tarot has 4 suits which vary by the region the cards come from. Each suit has 14 cards, and there is an additional 21-card trump suit and a single card known as The Fool.. There are major and minor arcana elements in every suit, though the minor arcana are considered optional for readings by some practitioners. The major arcana consists of the Trump cards and The Fool, while the minor arcana is made up of the ten pip and four court cards in every deck.

The major Arcana has 22 cards, each which represents a step in a journey from The Fool's ignorance to finding wisdom and unity within the universe. Because these cards represent a progression, it can help a reader to understand this progression -- that is, where each card comes from and where it goes.

The minor Arcana suits are Swords, Cups, Wands, and Pentacles. Pulling a Sword card usually means something interpretative of your inner thoughts, your words, or your actions. The Cups generally represent feelings, inspiration, and creativity. Wands typically have to do with spirituality and energy. Finally, Pentacles are drawn to indicate something about money, material things, or stability.

The minor Arcana is more specific and not as big-picture as the major Arcana cards in the deck. The elements are also represented by the minor Arcana. Wands are fire, Cups are water, Swords are air, and Pentacles are earth.

Some Tarot readers allow cards to be drawn upside down, which changes the meaning to an inverse one. However, many Tarot readers, from beginners to experienced diviners, prefer to play only upright Arcana cards.

Tarot typically involves two people - a querent, who is posing a question to the cards, and a reader whose job it is to interpret the meaning of the cards. The querent may choose to disclose their question or keep it to themselves. A skilled reader doesn't need to know the question to read the cards.

However, as you may know, sometimes the reader is also the querent. If this is the case, the reading becomes a little different, because the cards represent people differently. A well-practiced reader will notice patterns over long periods of times in the layouts of the cards; there may be one or several cards that the reader begins to associate with themselves or others because that card appears often to represent that person.

If the imagery speaks directly to you, that intuition is recommended to be followed rather than just using the standard imagery interpretations. The cards are intending to speak directly to the reader and the seeker, so anything personal is no coincidence. Let the cards have your own voice!

The cards are pulled in some order, referred to as a spread. Maybe a one-card draw to see how your day will go, or a three-card spread asking the universe about your crush. The cards should always be read in context with other cards pulled. The positioning of the cards may also be significant, especially in Celtic and Kabbalistic card patterns. Ask yourself, how did this card work with the last card I drew?

Many Wiccans keep a log of their readings in a journal. This journal may be very thorough, writing which cards were drawn, what imagery was important, what feelings were evoked, who was doing the reading and the seeking, and how one feels about the reading. This helps the Tarot to act as a mirror to the soul of the interpreter. It allows beginners to learn more efficiently, and experienced readers to keep track of their energy.

Conclusion

Wiccan practices, by nature, vary widely. There are, however, some commonly held beliefs, as we have covered, as well as festivals that most Wiccans observe. Wiccans who practice without magic celebrate the Sabbats throughout the Wheel of the Year and focus on gratitude to Mother Earth. Wiccans who practice magic still adhere to this nature-based orientation, focusing on the elements and the stars in their Craft. We can even interpret the forces of nature through divination and channel them through spells and magickal items.

The next chapter will focus on another vital component of Wiccan belief and practice, which is deity worship.

Chapter 3 Wiccan Deities and

The Afterlife

Wicca is a religion that predates Christianity, so the form of worship may be unfamiliar to many. Wiccans worship specific deities within a pantheon. These Gods or Goddesses may be worshipped in hopes of advancing some cause, or a God or Goddess may "choose" a Wiccan to worship them by sending them signs.

Who you worship and how is completely your choice in Wicca. The goal is to have the most natural relationship possible, to feel intimacy with the Divine influences that surround us all. During turning points in a Wiccan's spiritual life, a new Divinity may call to them. Some Wiccans feel that a certain deity has chosen them, rather than the other way around.

There are a few distinct patterns amongst Wiccans when it comes to belief and worship of deities. More traditional Wiccans, like Gardnerian Wiccans, are polytheists who believe in two "parts" of a universal God, a male part and a female part.

Other Wiccans subscribe to polytheism, where they believe in and sometimes worship multiple Gods from a wide range of mythologies and pantheons. Celtic, Greek, Egyptian deities -- polytheists are looking to connect with deities that appear to them naturally, no matter where their lore is originally from.

Still other Wiccans consider their worship to fall *within* Abrahamic tradition; they may believe in monotheism, or they may engage in the worship of female Abrahamic figures such as Mary. Wiccans may have vastly different interpretations of traditional scriptures, and may be considered heretics by mainstream society.

Duotheism: The Horned God And The Triple Goddess

Those who believe in The Horned God and the Triple Goddess are considered to be *duotheistic*, meaning they believe in a dual entity of God; the male and the female. Many Wiccans feel this explains the balance in the universe, as well as the conflicts where male and female fail to harmonize.

The Horned God represents the unity "between the Divine and animals", man being included in the definition of animals. The horns represent the dualistic nature of The Horned God. He is night and he is day, summer and winter. The two horns added to the triple aspect of the Goddess are often mapped as the five points of a pentagram.

The Horned God is connected with the forest, and is seen very much as a protector of the Goddess and all her sacred children. As duality demands, he both gives life and takes souls from the world with death. He is known as a loving God who guards creation.

The Triple Goddess, completing the duotheistic belief system, represents all Divine Feminine aspects of the universe. She is most often symbolized by the moon and the ocean. The Triple Goddess gets her name from the three stages of a woman's life: The Maiden, The Mother, and The Crone. Of course this is a very ancient tradition that no longer applies universally to all women, but regardless the Triple Goddess is a representation of all the positive and negative attributes of being a woman.

The Maiden represents enchantment and youth. This is a time of purity and new beginnings. The Greek Goddess Persephone is most often associated with The Maiden.

The Mother represents fertility, power, and stability. The Mother is the ultimate creator, the giver of life, the nurturing one. In Greek myth, Demeter is associated as the Mother, a compassionate and selfless giver.

Repose and wisdom are attributes of The Crone, along with the status of being an elder. Wiccans revere their elders, as they have had much more experience in interpreting signs, interacting with spirits, and creating effective rituals. The Greek Goddess Hecate is known as The Crone, with the satisfaction of a lifetime of knowledge.

POLYTHEISTIC PRACTICES

Other modern Wiccans are polytheists. This means that they *believe* that there are many or at least multiple deities. It doesn't mean they necessarily worship more than one deity, however; many Wiccans dedicate their practice to one or a few select Gods or Goddesses with whom they feel a special spiritual connection.

Wiccans draw deities from the lore of several different societies, including ancient Greek and Roman pantheons, along with pre-Christian European deities such as Norse myths or The Horned God. Wiccans may also spiritually access Egyptian and Hindu Gods and Goddesses.

Some Wiccans connect spiritually with their deities without naming them because their goal is to channel whoever is close and present. Other Wiccans, on the other hand, find that channeling a particular God or Goddess using certain ritual objects like candles, incense, and crystals is more effective for them. We will discuss how to begin channeling deities in Chapter 5.

Hellenistic Wicca: The Pantheon of Olympus

Hellenistic Wiccans are those who include the Gods and Goddesses from Greco-Roman mythology in their worship and practice. Greek and Roman imagery has been so ubiquitous in our society and culture that many feel it is part of the heritage of all Wiccans. Because of this constant exposure to these myths, some Wiccans feel more strongly connected to this pantheon than to others.

Looking at the pantheon of deities from Greek and Roman myth might seem a little overwhelming. But the pantheon is very compatible with Wicca. This is because each God or Goddess is associated with something in the natural world. Indeed, many of the Gods and Goddesses exist to explain the phenomenon of the natural world around us.

The "main" Greek deities are even associated with planets and elements, and can be connected to astrology as well. The five classical elements actually come from Hellenistic understandings of the world. Before that time, the elements were known as the earth, sky, and sea by the Celtic occult groups.

This level of nuance is highly conducive to the individualism encouraged in Wiccan practice. Another advantage of

Hellenistic Wicca is that unlike other European pantheons which have had much information lost to the ages, so much of the Greek and Roman lore remains intact and accessible. In fact, there may be no pantheon more complete or detailed than that of Greece and Rome.

Hellenistic beliefs are compatible with the Wheel of the Year as well. Many Hellenistic Wiccans associate the story of Persephone and Demeter with the Wheel of the Year, because it explains the coming and going of the seasons. The rise and fall of Dionysus, the Hellenistic God of harvest, wine, and celebration, is also associated with the Sabbats and festivals.

The 12 most important Hellenistic deities are as follows:

1. Jupiter/Zeus: King of the Gods, Zeus is the god of thunder and the sky.

2. Hera/Juno: Queen of the Gods, Hera is the patron Goddess of women and femininity.

3. Athena/Minerva: Born out of the head of Zeus, Athena is the Goddess of wisdom and strategy.

4. Poseidon/Neptune: Often depicted with a trident, Poseidon is the God of the ocean and freshwater, earthquakes, and horses.

5. Aphrodite/Venus: Aphrodite was born out of seafoam and is a maternal Goddess of sexuality, love, fertility, beauty, desire, and prosperity.

6. Ares/Mars: The son of Hera, Ares is the God of war, aggression, virility, and the protector of agriculture.

7. Apollo/Apollo: Depicted as powerful archer, Apollo is the twin brother of the Goddess Artemis and the God of healing, music, and truth.

8. Artemis/Diana: Daughter of Zeus and twin of Apollo, Artemis is the Goddess of the hunt, the moon, birth, rebirth, and is a protector of women and a symbol of virginity.

9. Hephaestus/Vulcan: The creator of the weapons of the Gods and Goddesses, Hephaestus is the God of the forge, metalwork, and volcanoes.

10. Hestia/Vesta: Known as the sacred fire of the Vestal Virgins of Rome, Hestia is the Goddess of the hearth, the home, and the family.

11. Hermes/Mercury: Son of Zeus and the guide of spirits in the underworld, Hermes is the God of communication, thieves, trickery, profit, and trade.

12. Demeter/Ceres: Known as the eternal mother, Demeter is the Goddess of agriculture, grain, marriage, motherhood, and marriage.

Celtic Reconstructionist Wicca

Many Gardnerian Wiccans use Celtic elements in their Craft. Other Wiccans who don't identify with a tradition may also choose this path. The founder of Wicca included many Celtic influences in his original rituals and belief system, and many who believe in the traditional ways laid out by Gardner have chosen to preserve these influences.

The Celtic Reconstruction movement, associated with Neo-Druidism, is an attempt to recreate ancient Celtic practices with as much historical and spiritual accuracy as possible. Celtic traditions have survived through folklore and songs, as well as through prayers passed down through generations.

Unlike other Wiccans, Celtics believe in the Three Elements: the Land, the Sea, and the Sky. Fire is viewed as a force of inspiration which unites the three realms, and not an element in and of itself.

Celtic Wiccans are focused on interacting with the Otherworld, and use divination and offerings to connect with the ancestral spirits of the land. Offerings include food, drink (usually alcohol), and art. Most Celtic Wiccans maintain altars to honor their patron spirits and deities, and in this tradition it is most common to place the altar outside. Ideally the altar would be near a well or a stream, or some naturally occurring water.

Some important Celtic deities include:

1. Brighid, The Goddess of the Irish Hearth. Revered as the Goddess of the hearth and the home, Brighid is also a Goddess of prophecy and divination. Brighid is the Triple Goddess in modern Wiccan tradition.

2. Cailleach, Queen of Winter. Sometimes known as the hag, Cailleach is the bringer of storms. Known as the Dark Mother of winter, Cailleach is also known for taking part in creation.

3. Cernunnos, Wild God of the Forest. Representative of the Horned God in modern Wicca, Cernunnos is the god of masculinity and fertility.

4. Cerridwen, The Keeper of the Cauldron. A Welsh Goddess, Cerridwen brews the cauldron of the underworld that is the source of ideas and inspiration.

5. The Dagda, The Irish Father God. Legend tells that the Dagda caused himself to lose his own powers. He is the father of the other Gods and Goddesses of the Celtic pantheon.

6. Herne, God of the Wild Hunt. An ancient English God, Herne is considered the God of the common people, as well as the God of vegetation and hunting. Herne is celebrated in the fall, when the deer go into rut.

7. Lugh, Master of Skills. Honored during the harvest festival of Lammas, Luch is the God of craftsmanship, blacksmithing, and artisans.

8. Rhiannon, the Welsh Goddess of Horses. Famed for her intelligence, Rhiannon is a Goddess of wealth and charity.

9. Taliesin, Chief of Bards. Interestingly enough, Taliesin is a real documented person who has been elevated to the status of a minor Celtic God. He is the patron of poets and musicians.

KEMETIC PANTHEON

Kemetic or Egyptian Wicca has a strong focus on the moon. Esbats are important events for them, and they gather in large groups to celebrate the moon as a community. These congregations are called temples rather than covens in this tradition.

The most important God in the Egyptian pantheon for Wiccans is Ra, the ancient God of the sun. During the day, Ra exists in the Overworld creating the sunlight and is depicted as a falcon with a sun disk around the head. At night, some legends say that Ra goes to the Underworld, and transforms to have the head of a ram, the horns representing the duality of day and night.

Ra is believed to originally been united as one being with Horus, the God of the sky. Together they made all of creation by speaking all creatures into existence using the secret names of their souls. Ra split off to rule over every domain: the sky, the earth, and the underworld.

Other important deities of this pantheon include:

1. Amounet is the Goddess of fertility and motherhood.

2. Anubis is the God of the dead and the process of preserving the body through embalming.

3. Atum is a deity that switches between male and female, and is considered to be the creator of Egypt. He rose from the waters of chaos to become the first God, who created the rest of the Egyptian Gods.

4. Bast is a Goddess of protection with the head of the cat. Originally the protector of the Pharaoh, she is gentle but a vicious enemy for those who threaten people under her protection.

5. Hathor is the Egyptian Goddess of happiness, and was considered to be the mother of the Pharaoh. In modern Wiccan practice she is worshipped as the mother of the home and domesticity.

6. Horus is the God who protects the Pharaoh, but was also considered to be incarnated in the Pharaoh. Horus lost an eye in battle, and since then the Eye of Horus has been an important Egyptian symbol of protection.

7. Isis is the mother of Horus. She is a Goddess of protection and maternal love and is often depicted nursing the infant Horus.

8. Ma'at is the daughter of Ra and the Egyptian Goddess of happiness, love, and justice.

9. Nun is the eldest of the Egyptian Gods. Before achieving form as a God, Nun existed as the primordial waters of chaos. He is the God of pre-creation.

10. Osiris is the God of the underworld, death, and the dead.

NORSE PANTHEON

Norse mythology is rich with dragons, giants, elves, dwarves vikings, and more. Though many details are lost to the ages, the tradition still lives on in Wiccan practice.

The ancient Norse folk were at times severe, but often playful as well. This playful nature is often lost in the Wiccan revival of Norse folklore and worship, traded for a focus on the warrior spirit. However, it is important to remember that the Norse ancestors weren't all kings and warriors seasoned from battle. The majority of them spent their lives performing difficult, physically demanding work and enduring cold, bitter winters. In remembering the truth about their lives, some Wiccans choose to honor their memory by engaging with the Norse pantheon.

Norse myth was transmitted through oral tradition, and by the time any of it was written down the area had already been dominated by Christians. There are two holy texts that preserve Norse legend, but they were written by Snorri Sturlason in the 1300s after he had already been converted to Christianity. Sturlason knew that if he wrote anything the church deemed as blasphemy, he could be sentenced to death. Thus, much of the true spirit of Norse religion has been lost to time.

The Eddas contain the words of the High One, a God known as Odin who is proclaimed as the "AllFather". The values of the Eddas include truth, honor, and a moral code based on loyalty. It is written that one should protect one's own family and possessions and retaliate severely against those who betray you. The Eddas also teaches about the importance of physical and mental strength.

There are nine Nordic worlds, which are held by the branches and roots of Yggdrasil, the tree of the world. Each realm houses different beings, such as animals (including humans), Giants, and Divinities. The Norse also believe in Ragnarok, or the day of destruction.

The Norse Gods and Goddesses include:

1. Odin is the Father of all Gods and humans. Often depicted wearing a floppy hat or a winged helm, Odin is a warrior God known for wisdom, magick, wit, and knowledge. Though he is known as a literal warrior, Odin also represents mental warfare, considering his cerebral qualities. Odin is associated with the astrological sign Sagittarius.

2. Thor is the son of Odin and the God of thunder, lightning, and strength. Thor is typically shown wielding his mighty hammer, Mjollnir. Rugged and powerful, Thor guards Asgard, the realm of the Gods. Thor is linked with the astrological sign Leo.

3. Freya is a Goddess known for love and beauty, but she is also a hyper-intelligent warrior. Freya guides the souls she chooses that are lost in battle to Valhalla, the Norse heaven. She and her twin brother Freyr are connected to the astrological sign Gemini.

4. Freyr, twin of Freya, is known as the God of the Elves. Freyr is a God of virility and fertility. His boar is a sacred symbol that is said to bring the dawn.

5. Tyr is the God of the ancient wars and the lawmaker for the Gods. Tyr is invoked to bring about justice and right action. Tyr used to be the leader of the Norse pantheon, but was replaced by Odin. There are no record that explain why this transition occurred. Tyr is associated with the astrological sign Libra.

6. Loki is a trickster God, known for his acts of chaos. While he challenges the structure and rules of Asgard,

his antics are necessary to bring about the change the world needs. Loki has demonic elements, and is associated with the astrological sign Aries.

7. Heimdall is a handsome God with golden teeth. His role is to guard the rainbow path that leads to the realm of the Gods. He holds the signal horn that is blown to warn the Gods of Ragnarok. Heimdall is linked to the astrological sign Aquarius.

8. Skadi is the Goddess of winter and the hunt. She is a Goddess of judgment, vengeance, and righteous anger. It is she who delivers Loki's banishment to the underworld. Skadi is represented by the astrological sign Capricorn.

Abrahamic Wicca

While some might see it as a contradiction or heresy, there are followers of the three Abrahamic religions that also identify with and practice Wicca. Abrahamic Wiccans believe that the one Abrahamic God controls all of existence, including the stars that guide astrology. An Abrahamic Wiccan would argue that if you pull a card from a tarot deck, the Abrahamic God controlled the outcome of which card appeared. Thus, Wicca can interpret the signs sent by the Abrahamic God through the universe.

Though all of the Abrahamic religions center around the same God, described by different prophets, there is much nuance and difference in the way they worship, practice, and perceive God. They also use different central religious texts.

All Abrahamic Wiccans believe in emulating the behavior of the prophets of God. Christians additionally focus on living a life mimicking the path of Jesus and his disciples. Muslims imitate the life of Muhammad, and Wiccans often include the behavior of the wives of Muhammad to provide feminine balance.

Many Abrahamic Wiccan women choose to cover their hair as a sign of devotion and remembrance of God. Jewish women honor God in this way by wearing *tichel*, which are wraps that go around the back of the head but do not cover the neck or face. Christian women often wear veils made of lace, or veils that wrap loosely around the head to show the hair but not the neck, in imitation of Mother Mary. Muslim Wiccan women wear the *hijab*, a veil that covers all of the hair as well as the chest and neck, or a *niqab* which also covers the face.

Jewish Wiccans focus on the Tanakh, or the Hebrew Bible as their central texts. This is known by Christians as The Old Testament. For Jewish Witches, God is known by a respectful title HaShem, which means simply "The Name". This is because outside of prayer and ritual environments, the names of HaShem are considered to be too holy to speak aloud. HaShem is called Adonai when called upon in prayer, but also has seven names which reveal more about the nature of the Divine.

A Jewish Wiccan would be most likely to practice Kabbalah, or the ancient art of Jewish mysticism. The Zohar is the book which explains how to begin to understand the complex and multilayered realms of Kabbalah. Kabbalah tries to understand the secret meanings of the Torah, often by using complicated numerology. Hebrew letters are also numbers, so the Torah can be interpreted by examining the patterns therein.

The most traditional Kabbalistic Jewish Wiccans believe that one cannot even begin to fathom the truths of Kabbalah until one has reached the age of 40. However, there are Kabbalistic tarot spreads and other methods of accessing the knowledge of Kabbalah before this coming of age occurs.

The Bible is the main holy text for Christian Wiccans, though The Old Testament is important for context as well.

Christian Wiccans often venerate the saints as well as the Virgin Mary. Mary represents the Divine Feminine. Calling from Wiccan influences, Mary represents all at once The Maiden, The Mother, and The Crone, being pure, maternal, and wise. This balances the trinity of God, which is the Father, the Son, and the Holy Spirit.

Christian Wiccans celebrate both Christian holidays and the festivals of the Wheel of the Year, mixing elements of both belief systems into each holiday. Christmas and Easter, as they are celebrated, actually already incorporate many pagan rituals such as tree-decorating and fertility symbols (e.g. eggs, rabbits).

There is also a large focus on returning to the roots of Christianity. This means being highly educated on the facts about the life of Jesus of Nazareth and what He stood for instead of taking someone else's word for it. Many Wiccans feel that Christianity has been wrongly warped from its original intentions and used as a device for war and division when it preaches about peace and unity.

The holy book of Muslims is called the Qu'ran. Qu'ran means "recitation" in Arabic, and recitation of the Qu'ran is extremely important to all Muslims. It is said that Allah gave the Qu'ran to the humans and the djinn (spirits), but not to the Angels. Thus, whenever one recites Qu'ran, the Angels draw in close to listen. You are encouraged to greet the Angels who peek over your shoulders when you finish your recitation.

There are different sects of Islam just as there are for every large religion. Most Wiccan Muslims are in a sect called *Sufism*. Sufism is Islamic mysticism. Islamic mysticism focuses on the power of trance and meditation, worshipping the divine feminine, and worship through music and dance. Whereas most Muslims harshly condemn magick, Sufis defy labels and many don't self-identify even as Sufis. Sufis believe in full capacity for spiritual growth in all directions.

WICCAN AFTERLIFE

After all that discussion about divinity, it seems only appropriate to address what Wiccans believe about the great beyond. While Abrahamic Wiccans may follow the afterlife beliefs of their own traditions, the majority of Wiccans believe in reincarnation and a realm called the Summerland.

THE CIRCLE OF REINCARNATION

Pulling from beliefs that predate the Abrahamic religions, most Wiccans don't believe in heaven or hell. These concepts did not exist in ancient religions, though they did have ideas about what happens after death. Many Wiccans believe that when you die, you are reborn again into the cycle of the cosmos.

Just as Wiccans believe in the Wheel of the Year and the cycles of the moon, reincarnation is just another cycle in the universe. We are born, we live, we die, and we are reborn again. Many witches believe in a karmic system, where what one does in this life will have a ripple effect through one's coming lives. Because of this, Wiccans take their actions very seriously, and do their best to lead kind, compassionate lives.

Wiccans believe we are put on this Earth to constantly be in a state of self-improvement. If you've ever known a Wiccan, you probably know there's a large focus to constantly be learning, reading, and discussing, as well as reevaluating ideals. This is often called the Great Work.

According to Wiccan legend, we are gifted more than one life in order to learn all that we can possibly know about nature and the cosmos. One life is not sufficient for this to occur. Each lifetime encompasses a set of lessons, and the universe has such a vast variety of lessons to teach each and every one of us. Indeed, each soul is unique and needs to learn different lessons at different times.

Once one has perfected this knowledge, after many, many lifetimes, one is released from the cycle of reincarnation and enters the Summerland, which is the topic of the next section. Apart from being an escape from reincarnation, the Summerland is also the place where the soul rests between incarnations. This is often a time to reunite with loved ones from all our different lives, should they happen to be in the Summerland at the same time.

For Wiccans, death is just another step in the eternal dance of the balance of the universe. The soul itself has no name, no gender, no race, no age, and is not a physical thing. It is a spark reflected from the deities, whichever one might follow. While the body may die, the soul will always live on; it is immortal.

When the soul visits the Summerland between incarnations, it is not a time of judgment but rather a time for weighing what has been gained and learned, and what lesson the soul will need to continue to grow in the next life.

The soul is able to see which lessons in the previous lives were heeded, and which were ignored. The soul reviews the previous life, with the insight of other spirits and deities that exist in the Summerland.

Some witches are able to access information about their past lives. There are several methods through which this can be done. Some witches receive information about past lives through dreams. These dreams may feature a guide, usually a spirit or deity, that shows the witch visions of the past. Spirits or deities may choose to do this if past knowledge will benefit the witch in the lessons of their current incarnation.

Others work to enter a trance state where this information is more readily accessible. It takes a great deal of discipline and practice to use this method. Trance work is part of the shamanistic tradition, and is not to be taken lightly. Witches should remember the persecution of witches that has existed for millenia, and be prepared to face some very difficult images and information. This kind of trance work is known as *journeying*.

So why would a witch want to seek information from a past life? Many witches believe that the key to understanding the deeper problems they face, mentally, emotionally, spiritually, and physically, lies in having an understanding of who we used to be. If a witch has issues making the same mistakes over and over in their current life, it could be a sign that they need to get in touch with their past lives to gain insight.

Because of their belief in reincarnation, Wiccans do not fear death. Wiccans don't view death as a release into oblivion, but rather as a door to birth and renewal. In your life, you meet your loved ones from past lives and get to know them again fresh, as strangers. This helps you to know the souls of your friends and family more completely, to form stronger and stronger bonds over the course of your various incarnations.

Some Wiccans believe in "soul groups" that gather and reincarnate together. These souls are deeply interconnected, and their lessons and knowledge-seeking requires every soul for completion. Some covens believe they have practiced together through many generations of incarnation.

Souls that have finished incarnating that remain in the Summerlands help the younger souls who still have things to learn. Within the Summerland there exists the Hall of Ancestors, where our ancestral souls who have finished incarnating feast and celebrate the beauty and joy of all they have learned and lived. These ancestors and spirits that remain in the Summerlands can be invoked or called upon for guidance by Wiccans in the mortal realm.

Because Wiccans believe in animism, and thereby believe in the souls of animals and other life forms, some Wiccans also believe animal souls enter and are reborn through the

Summerland. Animals are reincarnated as other animals, and complete their own spiritual journey that human beings cannot fully comprehend. For example, a dog may have been a lion in a past life.

THE SUMMERLAND

The Summerland is known by many names. Some call it Land of the Faerie, the Shining Land, the Otherworld, or Land of the Young. The Summerland is where the soul rests between reincarnations, and where a soul receives its final rest once the soul has completed its quest for knowledge in the mortal, earthly realms.

The concept of the Summerland is drawn, again, from the Old Religions. It is similar to the Celtic concept of Avalon. It also draws elements from the Roman and Greek concept of the afterlife, Elysium.

The Summerland is a realm, just like the one we inhabit during our lives, except it is much less dense than the realm in which living creatures dwell. This realm is neither heaven nor a hell-like underworld. There are two typical ways that the Summerland is envisioned by Wiccans.

The first way that the Summerland is visualized is a land of eternal abundance and summer. Wiccan souls in the Summerland escape the cycle of the seasons which include the loss and emptiness of winter, the rebirth and growth of spring, and the harvest of autumn. The Summerland from this perspective is a place with flowing, beautiful grassy fields where the gentle breeze soothes the soul after a long journey. There are peacefully flowing rivers. The soul finally unifies with all that is natural.

The second way the Summerland is conceptualized is a place without form. Souls interact directly, without bodies, communicating through and with the forces of the universe. The energies of souls are intertwined with the highest energies, those of the deities. Here one has a chance to unify with the identities of the celestial beings.

No matter which way one envisions the Summerland, its purpose is to prepare the soul for its new life. The process ages the soul in reverse; it becomes younger and younger until it is ready again to inhabit a new blessed infant. However, different souls may take more or less time to complete this process. That is to say, a soul that is 85 years old will not necessarily take only 85 years to grow young again.

Conclusion

As you might be able to tell by the wide variety of belief systems, Wicca is not a prescriptive religion. Wicca is a religion that encourages all seekers to find their own paths, and judgment from other Wiccans is highly frowned upon. There is not a right or wrong way to be a Wiccan. It is all about pursuing what calls to you, as long as that path does no harm to others.

Chapter 4: Wiccan Tools

Altars and Altar Tools

Wiccans maintain an altar. An *altar* is a sacred space cultivated by a Wiccan for meditation, prayer, offerings, spells, and divination. The altar can also be a space to connect with and worship deities. Altars are decorated with tools, crystals, art, and other things to make them unique and to help them channel the desired energies. Some Wiccans maintain multiple altars for different purposes.

The altar is the heart of one's sacred space. It is an area of concentrated energy, the seat of a Wiccan's worship. While in most organized religions the altar is found at the front of a congregation, inaccessible to the congregants, the altar in

Wicca is very personal. The altar is not shared with a whole community; it is a place for private worship and solitary devotion to the sacred.

Building your first altar can seem daunting, but it is an opportunity to create something completely unique. For some it is so intimidating that it is put off. Your altar doesn't have to mimic anyone else's or have significance to anyone except for you. As long as the items on your altar are meaningful to you, that is all that matters.

Conversely, over-excitement can lead to a crowded altar covered with distracting trinkets that will only serve to collect dust. You want your altar to contain useful things. Altars are dynamic as well; what may be useful on your altar at first may eventually have fully served its purpose and need to be replaced as your beliefs and Craft develop.

Before we look at the different types of altars, it is important to understand the tools of the altar and their purposes, significances, and uses. The four main tools of the altar are the athame, the wand, the chalice, and the pentacle, each representing a different element. These four tools appear in the minor arcana of tarot, known as Swords, Cups, Pentacles, and Wands in the deck. The next sections will cover other important tools as well.

Don't worry about collecting all the tools as a beginner. The point is to learn about these tools and understand their uses. No tools are necessary to practice Wicca, but as you develop your practice you're likely to begin accruing them.

ATHAMES

An athame is a special dagger used for magickal rituals. The athame often is double-edged, with a pointed, sharp tip. Athames should be used with great care to prevent harm during use. Respect the athame as you would any other kind of knife. The handle of the athame is often inscribed with symbols or sigils. These carvings can vary depending on which tradition the practitioner is a part of.

The purpose of the athames are not to cut things, but rather to direct energy during the ritual. Cutting is considered a mundane task, and athames are reserved for the sacred. The athame represents the fire element. It is used to cast circles by outlining their circumference. The athame wards off negative energies and spirits during magickal work.

BOLINES

A boline is a ritual knife used for more mundane tasks than the athame. Traditionally the blade is one-sided and straight, but it is becoming more and more common to find them in a crescent shape to invoke the moon and the Triple Goddess. The boline has a white handle rather than a black one, and is usually smaller than an athame. The boline is used to cut herbs and cord, and to carve wands and candles.

PENTACLES

While the pentacle and the pentagram are related, they are not the same. To use the words interchangeably is incorrect, and it is important to know the difference.

The pentagram symbol is a five-pointed star contained in a circle. It is a type of talisman and can also be worn as an amulet. The five points on the pentagram represent many things. They represent the five elements. For Wiccans who worship The Horned God and The Triple Goddess, the five points also represent the two horns of the God and the three forms of the Goddess.

However, a ritual pentacle is different from the simple symbol pentagram. The pentacle is drawn as a pentagram, but also includes other writing. A ritual pentagram is often the centerpiece of the altar. It can be used to summon spirits or energies. The pentagram can be made from many natural materials, such as wood or paper. Within the pentagram, the words and symbols of whatever is being summoned are drawn.

CHALICES

A chalice is a cup used for ritual purposes, often resembling a goblet. A chalice may be filled with wine, whiskey, beer, water, or a number of other fluids with magickal properties depending on what the ritual is for. The ancient Romans would drink from chalices at banquets and feasts, and at the dawn of Christianity chalices were used for ritual purposes.

The chalice represents the element of water, and represents the womb. If one worships a female deity, it could represent the womb of that deity and be used to encourage fertility. The base of the chalice represents the physical world. The stem of the chalice symbolizes the connection between the mind, the body, and the spirit. The rim is that from which we receive spiritual energy, if the chalice is used to drink from.

When used in combination with an athame, the chalice and the athame together represent the feminine womb of the Goddess and the masculine phallus of the God coming together to create.

Wands

A wand is a thin, straight carved piece of wood, ivory, metal, or even crystal. The wand is meant to be hand-held. Originally, wands were supposed to stretch from the tip of the middle finger to the elbow, but as tradition has evolved wands have become smaller. Wand traditions trace back to ancient Egypt, where wands were buried in tombs for souls to use in the afterlife. The Hellenistic God Hermes/Mercury is also depicted as having used a wand.

Wands are commonly carved from wood of sacred trees, such as willow, elder, and oak. However, with new technology wands can be made from many materials. Some modern wands are made entirely of crystal or have crystal tips attached.

While the most effective wands are handcrafted, store-bought wands also work if you feel a connection with them.

CANDLES

Candles are a primary tool for Wiccans, and their different colors are used for different purposes. During a ritual they are placed at the four corners of the ritual circle to represent the presence of the four elements Fire, Wind, Earth, and Water (Aether is represented by the practitioners themselves).

Candles can be consecrated and charged for use by cleansing and anointing them with concentrated essential oils. Always do your research before using an oil, because some are more flammable than others, and you don't want an out of control blaze on your hands. Many Wiccans also sprinkle dried herbs over the candles to invoke their properties.

The colors of the candles are very important to for rituals and spells. Luckily, candles can often be found for low prices at your local dollar store, or in bulk online. Below is a brief review of the various candle colors and what they represent and invoke.

White: unity; spiritual truth; strength; peace and purity; breaking curses; meditation; purification

Yellow: persuasion; creativity; confidence and charisma; improving memory and studying

Green: nature, renewal, and fertility; healing; money and prosperity; emotional soothing and balance

Pink: love and strengthening friendships; femininity; spiritual healing; warding away evil

Red: strength and vitality; power; sexuality; passion; protection; the cycle of reincarnation

Orange: strength, courage, and authority; concentration; encouragement

Blue: psychic powers and spiritual awareness; wisdom and intelligence; harmony and balance; dreams of prophecy; protection while sleeping

Purple: mysticism; ambition; inspiration and idealism; heightening psychic abilities; breaking curses

Brown: animal healing; protection of animals; attracting money; solving domestic issues; finding lost objects

Gold: masculinity; intuition; persuasion and charm; protection; gaining luck and fortune quickly

Silver: removing negativity and encouraging stability; neutrality; developing psychic ability

Black: loss, grief, disappointment, and sadness; depression; absorbing and destroying evil and discord; protection from retribution

If a spell calls for a candle color you don't currently have, white candles are often used as a neutral acceptable replacement. It helps to carve a sigil in the candle to endow it with the energy of the colored candle you are replacing.

INCENSE

Incense is another important tool for many Wiccans. Incense is a substance, usually found in the form of a stick of infused herbs, which can be burned to release a fragrant smoke. Thought to have originally been used by Egyptians, the practice spread far and wide, adopted by Romans and Greeks and pagans worldwide.

Incense represents four elements at once. It is created from materials from the Earth by soaking them in Water. Then it is ignited with Fire, upon which time it wafts smoke through the Air. Some Wiccans consider its connection to Air to be the strongest, because it is an aesthetic representation of Air and helps us see the movement of the air around us.

Incense is held in a special container called a censer. This can take many forms. It could be a flat, straight piece of wood or other material upon which the ash can fall. Some witches fill a ceramic or metal cauldron with coal and burn incense within the cauldron. For certain rituals, ashes are important, so often times the ashes are saved to use in other spells and rituals.

There is an enormous variety of incense to choose from, but there are definitely types that are more commonly used. Frankincense is used to invoke masculine power and the sun. It is burned to encourage deep spirituality and purification. Myrrh is similar in function to Frankincense, but is a feminine incense that also promotes healing. Pine and Cedar incense are used to cleanse a space. Copal is also used for cleansing, but is often used specifically to cleanse objects.

Another form of incense use is the use of dried bundles of white sage. The tips of the bundles are lit, while the user holds the base where the sage is tied together with string. The user then cleanses whatever needs to be cleansed. It could be tools, or a space. It is often used to dispel negative energies and spirits from entire houses, especially when one has just moved in. This process is called *smudging*.

TYPES OF ALTARS

One of the first steps to building your own altar is choosing what kind of altar you want. This will help you decide what should be present and what can be left out and used for other purposes.

SHRINES

A shrine is an altar created for the purpose of venerating a deity, or less commonly for ancestor worship. A shrine is the perfect place to pray, commune with your deity, and make offerings. Making offerings, such as flowers, herbs, or alcohol, brings you closer to the deity. Offerings also encourage the deity to guide you in general, or to help you with a specific task.

Shrines are typically simple, because they are a focal point and therefore should have a clear, focused energy. A representation of the focus of the shrine is usually used, whether it's a statue or a drawing or photograph. Candles are placed on the shrine to "activate" the energy of the shrine. Small decorations such as vases are good ways to keep fresh offerings present, and also a good way to remember Wiccan veneration of all that is natural.

Really, that is all that is necessary for a shrine. Simplicity is the name of the game with this type of altar. Of course, you can add stones, crystals, and other things that channel or remind you of the subject of your worship. You should carefully consider what you add, though, to prevent your shrine from looking like a New Age flea market display.

During Samhain, ancestral shrines are much more elaborate. Ancestral shrines are decorated with photos of the ancestor, as well as personal belongings of theirs. Seasonal decorations such as apples, pumpkins, and root vegetables are often piled high as offerings to the departed. For a Samhain shrine, color is also important. Rich deep colors that represent the end of fall are used such as black, gold, and burgundy.

RITUAL ALTARS

A ritual altar is more elaborately done because it includes the tools necessary to perform the ritual. Ritual altars are used for occasions such as Esbats or festivals. A full ritual altar often includes an athame, wand, cup, pentagram, and candles (often many of them in different colors).

As a result of all the tools that are usually present during a full-blown ritual, these altars are usually quite large and often temporary. Ritual altars are typically constructed outdoors, where the connection with nature is strongest.

WORKING ALTAR

A working altar is one prepared for functional, practical magickal use. While some work can be completed in a single session, other ritual sessions or spells may require you to return to the altar multiple times. Thus, these altars are often more permanent than ritual altars.

This type of altar should be extremely focused and contain no more pieces than is absolutely necessary for the work being done. Excess tools and trinkets will distract from the magickal work and divert energy to other places.

PERSONAL ALTAR

A personal altar is more permanent, although the pieces included on the altar will change over time as your needs change. This kind of altar is often elaborately decorated with images, cloths, photos, crystals, candles, incense, and flowers. A personal altar is used to generate the desired vibrations. It can be focused on one particular energy, but in this case it does not have to be.

With any type of altar one should be cautious of clutter. Don't hold onto items without meaning to you, or that have worn out their usefulness. It's easy to become attached to material things, but this is contradictory to the Wiccan path. It is not the material things a Wiccan owns that gives them power. The power comes from within. If you're having trouble with materialism, take time to enjoy nature and remember the true roots of Wicca.

CRYSTALS

Gemstones and crystals are commonly used by Wiccans to channel certain cosmic energies in their day-to-day practices, or on special occasions. This section will teach you about what energies are held by which crystals and gemstones, and will also discuss how crystals can be used in magic.

There are a large range of purposes that crystals can be used for in magic. Crystals can be worn in jewelry to help you guide a certain vibration into your life on the go, for example. Crystals are also commonly found on the altars of many Wiccans. Whether you're looking to be more creative, be luckier in your love life, or be more in-tune with nature, there's a gemstone that will match the needs of your practice at any time in your life.

All stones can be charged, just like spells or water. Stones are great vessels for energy, and can be charged in the light of the full moon or by the bright shining sun during the day. Stones can be cleansed in a variety of ways, but some stones may be corroded by water so it is important to research the physical properties of the stone.

Cleansing a stone is often done once a month during the full moon, simply by leaving the crystals and stones out in the moonlight to refresh and rejuvenate their energies. At other times of the month, stones can be cleansed by burning cleansing herbs, most commonly sage. The stone should be held over the smoke and usually an incantation is read.

Stones associated with the element of your Astrological sign or with elements that resonate strongly with you may be easier for you to channel with, but any Wiccan can still work with any stone. Stones can also be attuned to your entire Astrological chart (e.g. using Amethyst to heal your love life if your Venus is a water sign).

AGATE

Agate can have many unique appearances, but generally has lush gold or bronze bands rippling through this unique stones. Blues, whites, and purples are also common colors found blended into this earthy stone.

Being connected with the Earth elements and the brow chakra, Agate is a stone that helps focus the mind. It can relieve depression and give you more energy. If you're feeling down and out, and could use some stress relief, carrying agate with you, wearing it as jewelry, or placing agate on your altar are magic practices that could offer you relief.

AMETHYST

This well-known and often-used favorite comes in a deep purple color, and is known to be associated with the Astrological sign Aquarius. This violet quartz crystal is a stone filled with water energies.

Associated with the crown of the head, amethyst is a healing stone, often used in rituals to heal anxiety or mood disorders. Amethyst can also be used to help cleanse a ritual space of negative spirits or energies that might be present, making it the perfect crystal to keep in an altar.

BLOODSTONE

Bloodstone is usually an olive green color with brown speckles decorating it. This stone is also known for healing properties, and as a fire stone is associated with Mars and the sun.

Bloodstone is particularly useful for its fertility properties, so if you're looking to start or grow your family, or if you're intending to channel fertility for another person, this is a great option for you.

DIAMONDS

Diamonds are clear stones, with a foggy appearance when uncut and a very radiant, sparkly appearance when cut that catches the light from every angle. These stunning stones are associated with the Sun and fire energy.

Diamonds can be used for the classic reasons of encouraging cosmic encounters that lead to engagement and marriage, but are another great stone for the treatment of fertility issues as well. A diamond can be used to treat infertility in men or women, including treating impotence in the bedroom.

GARNET

This burgundy stone can resemble the deep red of blood, or appear more purple. Garnet is connected with the Goddess Persephone and the fire element.

Garnets are strongly connected with moon magic, and can be charged by being left out to absorb the energy from a full moon, blue moon, blood moon, etc. This stone is tied to the complexities of a woman's body, and can be used to encourage fertility and regulate the menstrual cycle. A charged garnet will also boost other stones present at an altar.

Hematite

While unknown to many outside of magic practice, hematite is a favorite amongst Wiccans. This gorgeous silver-colored stone has ties with fire and the planet Saturn.

Hematite is used for healing, and is especially potent for treating blood disorders, infections, and fevers. A protection stone, it is great to have around on you to ward off negative energy and to protect you from hostile spirits. As jewelry, this stone can increase psychic awareness and magic ability.

Jade

Jade is a peaceful stone that is typically known for its beautiful green hue, though it comes in other colors as well. Associated with earth elements, this stone is a symbol of serenity.

Jade can be used to channel calmness, true love, and innocence. Jade is also used to balance the humors of the body in the liver and spleen.

JASPER

Jasper has a red-brown marble color, often with flecks of white mixed in. Associated strongly with earth elements, this stone is perfect for Tauruses, Virgos, and Capricorns.

Jasper can be used in rituals to ground and center your magic and your mind, perfect for concentration when working on spells or studying. It also has healing properties, specifically good for cancer treatment. You can also place a piece under your mattress to bring an extra spark to your love life!

LAPIS LAZULI

This stone may not be as shiny as some others, but the range of blues from light cerulean to deep royal blue make it undeniably elegant. Lapis Lazuli is often spotted or banded, depending on where the stone originally grew.

Lapis Lazuli is known to alleviate depression and soothe the mind. It is the best stone for meditation and trance exercises.

MOONSTONE

A soft opalescent milky white, moonstone has magical connections with -- you guessed it! The moon. It also is connected with lunar deities, and the number three. Any

Wiccan who is working with the number three or worships a deity involved with the number three will find use out of this brilliant stone.

This is another great stone to charge under special moon events. Because the moon is associated with femininity, this stone can be used to promote fertility and regulate the menstrual cycle. In terms of magical qualities, moonstone can help you get in touch with your wisdom when you need it the most. Moonstone is also great for intuition, and is the perfect stone to keep present at a tarot reading or other divination project.

Quartz Crystal

Quartz crystals are clear, but often have small milky flaws in them. Wiccan highly value these flaws, and for this reason a "crystal ball" should always be made from quartz rather than glass. The unique flaws in a Quartz are capable of snagging onto passing energies, which makes them useful in a spherical form or in a pendulum shape for divination.

Clear Crystal Quartz is an all-around positivity stone, and is very commonly worn in jewelry. The stone gives positive energy, general cleansing, and has gentle healing properties. It is an excellent stone for beginners who may feel overwhelmed by the energy of more powerful stones.

Rose Quartz

The Rose Quartz is a fan favorite amongst Wiccans, both for its beauty and its gentle energy. Like Quartz Crystal, Rose Quartz is valued for its flaws and the variety of patterns in which it can manifest. Rose Quartzes are a soft rosy pink. Some are more clear, while others have a pink milky swirl within them.

Rose Quartz can be used to promote happiness, for new or deeper love, to help encourage forgiveness, and to bring about peace. It is a symbol of love and healthy relationships. The love radiated by a Rose Quartz is not only love for and from others, but love for the self as well.

Tiger's Eye

Tiger's Eye is a warm golden stone with deep brown streaks that go all the way through the length of the stone. The gold has a very distinctive shimmer in the light, and is quite a sight to behold. Tiger's Eye is a strong stone for protection.

The main purpose of Tiger's Eye is to give oneself clarity. Tiger's Eye helps you see through illusions, and helps you to identify the truth. This stone can also help us learn inner truths about ourselves.

TURQUOISE

Known for its striking bright blue with veins of brown, Turquoise is strongly associated with the astrological sign Sagittarius. Turquoise is another stone that promotes complete positivity. Turquoise is known for attuning to its user, focusing their energy wherever it is needed most.

This is the ultimate stone for healing. It promotes emotional, physical, mental, and spiritual well-being. It neutralizes negative energy and provides strong protection. It also promotes joy, friendship, and relaxation.

GRIMOIRES: A WITCH'S DIARY

A *grimoire* is often simply explained as a spellbook. Indeed, grimoires are often used to collect information about how to perform spells properly for easy, quick reference and access. While you can buy one, it is encouraged to eventually move on to create your own that is specific to your needs for your practice.

Also known as a Book of Shadows, this journal contains more than just spells. This is a place where Wiccans collect all their knowledge of the Craft for easy reference. Grimoires often contain information about herbs, crystals, astrology, moon cycles, and much more. This book is a Wiccan's go-to resource for their Craft.

Because of the critical focus on nature, Wiccans are constantly learning about the world around them. This often includes having a wide range of knowledge about natural materials, their correspondences, and their uses. Any magickal information may be recorded in a grimoire.

Wiccans have widely different traditions about how to create a grimoire. Many covens have specific rules and layouts to follow. This often includes consecrating the grimoire to endow it with sacred energy, and cleansing the book of any energy it may have previously held. Some Wiccans choose to mask the information by using codes, cyphers, or symbols to prevent the grimoire from being used by others.

Your grimoire should be created following your own intuition. If you want to use symbols and codes, that's your own decision. What you choose to write in your grimoire is also done at your own discretion.

In today's modern age, many choose to create a grimoire online using any of the multitudes of journaling software available. The benefit to this method is that the grimoire would be searchable by keywords, and it could have a password protecting its contents. This option is great for having your grimoire on the go without needing a physical copy.

Many people feel discouraged by poor handwriting or less than perfect art skills, and a digital grimoire offers a creative way to collect information without needing technical crafting skills.

Another method especially good for beginners is to create a binder. This allows you to move pages around or remove them without damaging the book. You can add dividers to separate clear sections to find things easily. For those without artistic ability, this is a good option because you can create and print out your own pages to go in the grimoire. For example, you can include photos of herbs and plants to help identify them alongside information about their medicinal and magickal properties.

Finally, a grimoire can be made from a bound journal. Often, these journals are decorated with magick symbols such as the symbol of the Triple Goddess. Some like to glue small flat crystals to the front, and to press flowers and herbs between the pages.

For beginners, many experienced Wiccans recommend starting two grimoires. One is the "final" grimoire, which contains your best art and your finest handwriting. The other would be a draft of a grimoire, where messiness is allowed. This allows you to experiment with the order of your entries and practice what you would like to write and draw before making it "official". Another method of having two grimoires is to have one for day-to-day witchcraft, and one for special occasions.

The most common advice given to beginners is not to take the grimoire so seriously that you are afraid to begin. The grimoire should come naturally. It is something to enjoy and cherish, not a chore or obligation. Work at your own pace, and experiment with different methods to find out what is right for you.

HERBS

Herbalism, or the study of the medicinal and magickal properties of herbs, is very popular amongst Wiccans. Wiccans believe herbs are not only beneficial because of their own characteristics, but also because they are endowed with the energy of the Earth. Each herb has unique uses, and Wiccans utilize them in a variety of ways.

It is important here to note that although Wiccans practice herbal remedies, this is not a replacement for professional medical treatment. It is a supplementary practice rather than a replacement for modern medicine.

Wiccans use herbs as natural remedies for minor pains and conditions, like headaches or indigestion. Many herbs can be made into teas or used to season food. Some Wiccans enjoy creating their own tea blends. Consuming an herb can also help you channel the magickal properties of that herb. For example, saffron is thought to boost creativity and is often enjoyed as a tea with a rich red hue.

Some Wiccans choose to grow their own herbs to connect with the earth and the Wheel of the Year. Many herbs can be grown indoors, if a garden is not available. Herbs are traditionally harvested in the morning, before the heat of the day sets in but after the sun has dried the dew from the plants. Harvested herbs can be used fresh in cooking, or hung upside-down to dry. Dried herbs can be used in kitchen witchery, and also can be burned in small quantities as incense.

The three most commonly used herbs in witchcraft are rosemary, thyme, and lavender. These three are considered essentials, although all herbs have their own unique values. They can be used fresh, dried, as incense, or as an essential oil. Here's what you need to know about the big three.

Rosemary

Rosemary is associated with the Sun and the astrological sign Leo. The primary correspondences for rosemary are creativity, wisdom, vitality, healing, protection, purification, love, strength, and stress relief. Rosemary is also known to provide mental clarity and confidence.

Rosemary is an acceptable substitute for Frankincense, an herb that grows in few climates and tends to be expensive. Rosemary can also be placed under a pillow to promote new ideas and creativity. A rosemary bath provides invigoration and positive energy.

Thyme

Thyme is associated with Mercury and Venus, as well as the element water and the astrological signs Taurus and Libra. Thyme makes a delicious tea. The primary correspondences for thyme are beauty, courage, psychic knowledge, healing, love, and purification. Thyme is also known to be very grounding, and can help avoid conflict.

Thyme is a favorite herb of the Fae. Planting thyme in your garden or home may attract them, so be sure to keep the thyme plants healthy! Faeries can be tricksters when they're displeased.

LAVENDER

Lavender is associated with the planet Mercury, the element air, and the astrological signs Gemini and Virgo. Its fragrance is very gentle and relaxing, and because of this it is often used to create "dream pillows". Dream pillows have lavender in their stuffing to help you fall asleep and to cast away bad dreams.

Lavender's primary correspondences are love, beauty, protection, relaxation, sleep, and psychic knowledge. Lavender is a lovely addition to bath water, to fully appreciate its lovely fragrance and to take time to unwind after a long day.

FAMILIARS SPIRITS: ANIMAL COMPANIONSHIP

Recorded accounts of familiar spirits go back to the Medieval ages, and the practice itself certainly existed before it was ever written down. A familiar is an animal, usually small, that acts as a companion and spirit guide. However, almost any animal can serve as a familiar.

In Wiccan history, witches who worked with familiar spirits were severely persecuted. A familiar was speculated to be a demon or some other evil paranormal force that could shape-shift into the form of an animal. Familiars were thought to serve witches by spying for them and cursing their enemies. All familiars were assumed by Christians to be malevolent.

Witches in the Middle Ages were often ostracized, marginalized, and lonely. For this reason, many began to keep small pets around for companionship. During the witch hysteria of the Middle Ages, owning a black cat was sufficient enough reason for extensive investigation into a woman's life.

Familiars were often used as evidence in witch trials in 16th and 17th century in England and Scotland. Leviticus, the third book of the Old Testament, mentions familiar spirits by name, and calls for anyone who works with familiars to be stoned to death. Thousands of women were executed, many of them having no connection at all with Wicca.

For the modern-day witch it is a happy blessing to gain this kind of bond with an animal. Keeping a familiar is a way for witches, especially those in the city, to cultivate a rapport with nature. Animals are much more in-tune with both natural and supernatural phenomena. Animals are sensitive to weather, and will often begin to act strangely if malevolent spirits are present.

By developing a relationship with a familiar, one can strengthen psychic abilities. The familiar can act as a medium between this world and the next. If you are attuned to the body language of your pet, you can recognize when supernatural beings are nearby.

OTHER WICCAN TOOLS

There are several other more minor, but still important tools that Wiccans use regularly.

Bells are an important Wiccan tool. As you start to read and learn about spells, don't be surprised to find that many include the ringing of a bell several times. Bells mark a transition in a ritual. A bell is often rung to begin and end a ritual, and may also be used throughout the ritual if the ritual has multiple steps.

Cauldrons are real, yes, and used by Wiccans in the Craft. They are probably the most well-known Wiccan tool, but there are many misconceptions about what they are used for. The optimal material for a cauldron is ceramic or cast iron, because they are intended to withstand large amounts of heat. Cauldrons can be filled with materials for a potion, for example, with a fire burning under the cauldron to warm and activate the ingredients. They can also be filled with small coals and used to burn herbs and incense.

Brooms are another commonly known Wiccan tool, but they aren't used for flight as seen in cartoons and movies. Wiccans use brooms to symbolically sweep away lingering energies. Because it is used for this ritual purpose, brooms are often handmade.

Finally, bowls are a simple and easily accessible tool for any Wiccan. Bowls are used to hold water (rainwater is best but any naturally occurring water may be used), salt, petals, herbs, or any number of other ingredients.

CONCLUSION

After all this discussion of the tools of the Craft, it is important to remember as a beginner that absolutely none of these tools are a requirement. Wicca is about communing with nature. Communing with nature attunes your natural abilities.

If you don't have access to tools yet, take advantage of the natural world around you. Go outside, visit a park, go on a hike, admire the mountains and the sea, meditate over the flow of the rivers, absorb the light of the sun and the moon, take time to stargaze. There are plenty of ways to connect with your inner Wiccan without spending any money at all.

Chapter 5: Practicing Magic

Once you feel in touch with nature and your inherent ability, it is wise to start learning about and practicing beginner magick. There's no need to rush into elaborate, confusing rituals with ingredients you've never heard of. With practice and patience, you will feel more in tune with your abilities. As you start to explore, you will eventually learn what elements of the Craft suit you best. Experimenting is important in early phases. The best way to learn is to read and put your new knowledge into action.

This chapter focuses on two things. The first is education. Even if you're not ready for spells yet, learning about them is the first step. Secondly, this chapter endeavors to teach you beginner's magick that is simple, effective, and harmless.

Magick and the Physical World

While Wiccans believe we all are born with inherent magickal talents, these talents are not absurd fictional miracles. There's no spell that will change the color of your eyes or make you taller, no spell that can create something from nothing. When learning about your talents and abilities, it is important to remember to be realistic. While some Wiccans have talents that are certainly spectacular, they operate within the laws of science.

Due to Wiccan reverence for nature, there is also Wiccan reverence for science. Wiccan beliefs do not contradict scientific findings. On the contrary, Wiccans are motivated to learn about science to deepen their understanding of the natural world, how it was formed, and most importantly how to preserve it.

Interestingly, scientific advancement has confirmed much that witches already knew. Witches of old had an intuitive understanding of the energy of all things, in addition to a wide range of knowledge regarding herbal medicine. Older scientific views perceived mind and matter to be separate completely (recall the phrase "mind over matter"). Witches have always known that mind and matter are one and the same, and of course science has confirmed that the mind functions because of the mechanisms of the brain, which is made of physical matter.

The brain is a powerful organ, and the power of thought is not to be underestimated. Thought-based practices, within Wicca but also in traditions like Buddhism that promote meditation and mindfulness, have been proven to cause actual positive change in our lives. Wiccans promote a focus on the positive, and cleansing of that which is negative. However, that is not to say that changing the way we think is a simple endeavor.

The Hermetic Principles or Hermetic Laws are a set of ancient laws that are important to Wiccan practice. We will not cover all of the seven principles here, because it is not obligatory to know them, especially for beginners, but we will touch on the most important ones and their basis in science.

An important Hermetic Principle is the Law of Attraction. This law simply states that positive thinking encourages positive outcomes. Part of the reason for this is because when we are in a positive state of mind, we are more likely to be aware and in control of our emotions and behaviors. Magick is of course, more complex than thinking positively, but regardless there is a sound psychological basis for this principle within modern scientific understandings of the brain and behavioral psychology.

The most emphasized Hermetic Principle in Wicca is called the Law of Correspondence. If you've ever heard the Wiccan phrase "as above, so below", this law is the basis for that saying. This means that whatever affects the macrocosm of the Universe in turn affects the microcosm, and vice versa. Some scientists refer to this as the Butterfly Effect. The Law of

Correspondence also teaches us that time is only one dimension, in a Universe that experiences neither time nor space.

Because the Law of Correspondence teaches us that the Higher Planes and the Lower Planes are interconnected, intentions are very important when conducting magick practices. Whatever energy you put into the Universe may have a great effect, and may even be harmful to another, which is against the Wiccan creed.

Modern physics has discovered that at the atomic level, all material things are composed of matter and energy. This is compatible with the Hermetic Law of Vibration. All atoms vibrate and therefore constantly emit energy. Atoms vibrate at different frequencies, which creates the different states of matter (solids, liquids, and gases).

We perceive colors because of the phenomena of vibration. Light vibrates at different frequencies, which creates the spectrum of color. Witches can and do pick up on and use these different energies in their practice. By understanding the energy of the world around us, Wiccans tune into that energy and are able to connect it to their own personal energy. Wiccans can also use this energy conversely to communicate with the energy of the Universe.

Chakra therapy is based on this understanding of color (amongst other things). Aligning one's chakras is a way to rebalance one's energy to reap spiritual and physical benefits.

Because the physical world involves so many complex variables, it is impossible even for physicists and other scientists to accurately account for every unknown. The same is true for Wiccans. Spells and rituals may go awry due to forces that had not been accounted for.

MOON PHASES AND LUNAR EVENTS

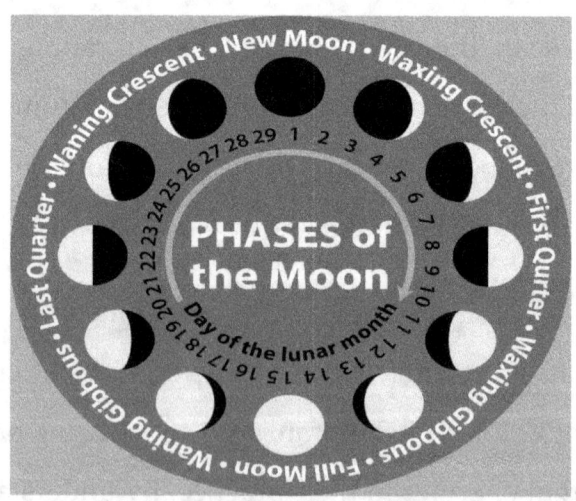

Whether or not you feel a significant connection to the moon, the phases of the moon have an effect on the magickal abilities of Wiccans. Different phases of the moon call for different phases of reflection. When the moon is full, the time is ripe for magick. It is best to keep a lunar calendar or use an app with reminders, to be aware of how the moon may be affecting you.

The cycles of the moon represent, for traditional Wiccans, the life cycle of women embodied by the Triple Goddess. The Triple Goddess in the form of the moon experiences birth at the new moon, and completion at the full moon. When the moon is waxing, or growing brighter, a Wiccan's power is growing stronger day by day. The waxing moon symbolizes the Goddess's journey from Maiden to Mother. When the moon is waning, it is time for Wiccans to rest, reflect, study, and prepare for the next lunar cycle. The waxing moon represents the Goddess's journey from Mother to Crone.

The new moon is a time to think about your goals for the coming month. It is a time of reflection rather than a time for action. The next moon phase, the waxing crescent moon, is a time to begin creating plans on how to achieve those goals. The first quarter moon is when Wiccans can begin to move towards these goals and think creatively. The waxing moon is a time of significant power, where Wiccans are in harmony with the forces of nature and prepare the rituals for the coming full moon.

During the full moon, there are many things that can be done. Crystals, water, and other magickal tools can be set out for cleansing and to charge with lunar energy. If you work with a group, consider having an esbat to celebrate, socialize, and practice together. If you are a solitary witch, the full moon is a perfect time to perform spells, enchant objects, or do any other important magickal work. Don't forget in all the hustle and bustle to stop and enjoy the beauty of this special evening!

During the waxing period of the moon, celebrate all you have achieved that month. Remember that every day you become wiser, even as the magick of the lunar cycle winds down. Let go of the past, and understand that mistakes are opportunities for growth. During the dark moon, remember that all things happen in their own time. Banishing spells are strongest during the dark moon, but take great care. The spell may be more powerful than you realize, and someone you could have reconciled with may disappear from your life permanently.

A lunar eclipse occurs when the moon is completely covered by the shadow of the Earth. While logic may tell us this would make the moon appear dark, the moon actually turns a magnificent, ethereal red color. It is a reflection of a million sunrises. This is often referred to as a blood moon.

Some Wiccans believe that during a total lunar eclipse, the moon represents every part of its cycle at once. This is because in a single night you can watch the Earth's shadow turn the moon through every phase, a complete waxing and waning. This effect is useful for multi-part spells that might otherwise have to be spread out throughout a month.

About every two or three years there comes a month where the moon will be full twice. This second full moon is known as a blue moon. This is the origin of the phrase "once in a blue moon". That saying has significance to Wiccans. A blue moon is thought to be twice as powerful as a full moon, and therefore magick can be performed that could only happen once in a blue moon.

CHAKRAS: BALANCING MIND, BODY, AND SPIRIT

Chakra is a sanskrit word meaning "wheel". Chakras are energy centers that are associated with an area of the body. Each chakra is associated with a color, and certain abilities and bodily functions. If your chakras are unbalanced, you may feel spiritually blocked. This happens even to experienced Wiccans. The trick is learning to identify the symptoms of imbalance. Chakras are also associated with physical and mental ailments, but aligning your chakras is not an adequate replacement for professional medical attention.

The concept of chakras comes from ancient Indian Hinduism, as well as Japanese, Chinese, and Tibetan Buddhism. The tradition was introduced to the West by renowned psychologist Carl Gustav Jung.

Chakra blockages can develop from trauma, negative experiences, unhealthy beliefs, insecurity, or self-doubt. The day-to-day stresses of life also gradually misalign the chakras. Chakra alignment can be done several ways, and is actually quite simple. It is an excellent way for a beginning Wiccan to get in touch with their mind, body, and spirit.

There are seven main chakras and signs of imbalance:

1. Root Chakra. An unaligned root chakra will cause you to have difficulties meeting your basic needs. The color of the root chakra is red, and it is located at the front of the body near the pelvis.

2. Sacral Chakra. Imbalance of this chakra manifests as confusion or difficulty with sexuality, and infertility. Its color is scarlet, and it is located in the lower abdomen near the stomach.

3. Solar Plexus Chakra. This chakra is linked to unhealthy eating habits, substance abuse, and depression. The

color associated with it is yellow, and it is located above the belly button and below the sternum.

4. Heart Chakra. Signs of imbalance of the heart chakra include difficulty with love, relationships and compassion. Its color is gold, and its location is the center of the upper chest.

5. Throat Chakra. The throat chakra is associated with your inner voice and your ability to communicate. Imbalance can cause anxiety, nightmares, and a fear of speaking your truth. Its color is blue-green, and it is located on the front base of the neck.

6. Third Eye Chakra. Symptoms of imbalance with this chakra may cause a lack of inspiration, problems sleeping, and psychic misinterpretations. The color associated with the third eye chakra is indigo, and it is located above and between the eyes, on the forehead.

7. Crown Chakra. The crown chakra is associated with inspiration and oneness with the cosmos. Imbalance may cause a loss of spiritual direction, headaches, confusion, and worry. Its color is violet, and it is located at the top of the head, slightly to the back,

The simplest way to align your chakras is through meditation. This is a visualization exercise, but it is important not only to "see" but to feel the energies as well. First, sit up straight and allow your shoulders to fall in a relaxed position. Relax and prepare with some deep breathing. Next, imagine whichever chakra you wish to balance as an orb. The orb should be the color of the chakra. Then, breathe deeply and imagine each breath fills the orb up until it is the size of a beach ball. Acknowledge and cope with any emotional pain you may find.

If meditation isn't your thing, each chakra can also be aligned by communing with nature or engaging in a meaningful activity that exercises that specific energy. Wearing the color of the chakra and/or eating foods associated with that chakra will also restore balance.

The root chakra can be aligned by taking care of your physical body. Remember to exercise and get adequate rest. Working in a garden or making art with clay such as pottery will also align this chakra. Red foods like beets and pomegranates can help, too.

In order to balance the sacral chakra, it is best to seek an encounter with natural water. This could mean swimming in a lake, ocean, or river. It could also mean walking in the rain or watching a storm. Oranges and carrots are good options to align this chakra.

Balancing the solar plexus chakra is done through education. Read a book, take a class, do a crossword puzzle. Sunshine can also balance this point of energy. Chamomile and lemon teas are useful as well.

The heart chakra is balanced by nature walks and quality time with family and friends. Nurture your relationships and express love. Ginger is a wonderful remedy for the heart chakra.

Your throat chakra can be balanced by singing, doing creative writing, and having important, deep conversations. Blueberries nourish the inner voice associated with the throat chakra.

The third eye chakra is most effectively balanced by taking time to go stargazing or walking in the light of the moon. Keeping a journal can also balance your third eye chakra. Associated foods are figs and black currants.

Finally, to balance the crown chakra, try getting in touch with your dreams. This means both the dreams you have while asleep and your goals in life. Keep a dream journal or make a vision board to regain your direction. Plums, lavender, and amethyst are useful in restoring balance to this center of inspiring energy.

Keeping your energies in balance will help you achieve harmony on the inside and the outside. If you've never balanced your chakras before, it is recommended to do so before you begin practicing Wicca. If your energies aren't in sync, your spirit won't be either, and you won't be able to properly focus your magickal senses.

Spells

Spells are magickal rituals that require symbolism, specific materials, incantations, concentration, and faith. The purpose of spells is to channel energy to enact some kind of change in a situation. For example, an author experiencing writer's block may perform a spell for creativity.

Spells date back to ancient Egypt and the Zoroastrian Magi, who influenced the activities of Roman and Greek pagans. Ancient Norse traditions also included this sort of ritual magick.

Spells can be directed at the self or at another, and can be positive or negative. However, performing negative magick against someone else goes against the Wiccan rede to do no harm. In fact, it is unwise to cast any sort of spell on someone else without their informed consent. Positive spells are sometimes called "blessings", or more archaically "enchantments". Negative spells are known as "hexes" or "curses".

Spells follow a specific formula in order to achieve the desired magickal effect. While the formula is important, what is most important is your intention and focus. It is impossible to cast a spell you don't believe in. Remember to be patient as a beginner, because your abilities may not be honed enough to cast certain spells.

One important rule when doing any kind of magick but especially spells is to pull energy from sources around you. If you pull energy from only your own resources, you will often feel drained, lethargic, and sometimes even hungry. This is the reason spells typically involve tools, but energy can also be drawn from nature itself.

Regardless of what spell you choose to perform, there are steps you should take to prepare for the ritual beforehand. The first step is to prepare your body and your mind. It is recommended to bathe before performing a spell. Some witches anoint themselves with relevant oils. If you have a special attire you prefer to use to perform magick, make sure the clothes are clean. Take time to meditate to relax and focus the mind.

If you are working indoors the next step is to cleanse your workspace. This can be done using crystals, by sprinkling salt around the perimeter, or by smudging (burning) white sage. Other options sprinkling rainwater or water purified by the full moon. Clear the clutter from the area in which you plan to work so there will be no interfering energies or distractions.

Now it's time to draw your circle. Not all Wiccan traditions do this, but it is the dominant tradition. The circle is meant to channel energy from the four cardinal directions. Water is represented by the North, Air by the East, Fire from the South, and Earth from the West. Creating a circle consecrates the space. You can trace the circle with your finger or a wand or athame, or you can physically draw one. Inside the circle, draw a pentagram. This circle is called a pentacle.

What happens after this varies from spell to spell. As a beginner, you can learn spells from reputable sources online (beware of phonies), but eventually you will have enough knowledge to begin writing your own spells.

Spells typically have an incantation, or a spoken verse that invokes your desires. It is common for these verses to rhyme. The incantation can invoke a deity, or even a planet or the moon for assistance. Incantations should be finished with the phrase "so mote it be".

Spells typically end by casting off a symbolic item. It could be burning a sigil (see next section), burning herbs, or something as simple as snuffing out a candle. Do keep in mind that you should never blow a candle out if possible. There are special devices made to snuff candles, but you can also use sand or water.

The final part of a spell is giving thanks. This could be an expression of gratitude to nature or any spirits or deities you invoked to aid you.

SIGILS: THE CONDUITS OF INTENTION

Sigils are symbols that represent an intention. Commonly used for protection, sigils require activation. Some sigils can be activated merely with focused intention. Other Wiccans prefer to burn copies of sigils to release their energy. Sigils are considered to be a basic, easy form of magic, perfect for beginners.

While you can easily find sigils for anything you could think of online, creating sigils is typically considered a very personal thing. Creating your own sigils is easier than you think, and can actually be fun and meditative.

When creating your sigil, make sure you are in a calm, quiet place with minimal distractions. Because sigils are manifested intentions, it is important that you completely focus on your intention during the process of creating or carving a sigil. If you become distracted, it is highly recommended that you start from the beginning.

To create your own sigil, you must first decide what your intention is. Your intention should be put into the form of a short, simple sentence. For example, "I am safe and calm". Once you have your sentence, depending on your tradition, the vowels may be removed from the sentences. From the remaining consonants, use each only a single time in your sigil. For the sentence used as an example, the consonants used would be "m, s, f, n, d, l".

The next step is your opportunity to get creative and truly connect with the sigil. Using the remaining consonants from your intention sentence, begin to create a shape by connecting and overlapping the letters. You can make the letters into simpler shapes like swirls, lines, and circles. When you feel you have created a shape that represents your intention, you are finished.

It's fine if you don't like your first try. It's common for witches to take their time drafting different versions until they are satisfied with the aesthetic of the sigil. By drawing your own sigil, the sigil contains elements of your personal energy and can be more effective.

You can carve sigils into candles and burn the candle to activate the energy of the sigil. Some Wiccans use sigils in cooking. For example, a kitchen witch may draw a sigil on the bottom of a pie crust to infuse the pie with protective energy and love. Another easy way is to draw a sigil in a cup using honey before pouring tea over it. Some witches draw sigils in their private notebooks to protect them from prying eyes.

BATH MAGICK

Bath magick is a fun and easy way to begin performing rituals. It has the benefit of doubling as a form of self-care, which promotes self-worth and self-love. Loving the natural world includes loving oneself, as Wiccans believe we are united with nature. Cultivating a positive opinion of yourself will also increase your confidence in your abilities, and empower you to continue seeking knowledge and improving your craft!

Different bath products have different magickal uses. The ingredients used are important, but there are very few bath products made with ingredients that would manifest a bad result. Either way, researching the components of your bath products is a great way to begin committing correspondences to memory. Handmade bath products are better than those produced by machines, but use whatever is available to you.

Bath salts can be used when you want to cleanse your spirit and your subconscious mind. Both salt and water have purifying qualities. Bathing with salts is an excellent way to prepare for a spell. Bubble baths are useful for when you want to be immersed in something in the conscious mind. Being surrounded by bubbles is symbolic of being submersed in your desires, thereby willing positive things into existence. This is sometimes called manifesting.

Bath bombs symbolically explode to push something rapidly into existence. Maybe you want to be kinder, or more spontaneous. This is a high-energy way to manifest your intentions. Bars of soap are great for carving sigils in. Thoroughly washing your body in the soap also covers you with your intentions, and the lingering scent will carry those intentions with you throughout the day.

You can also add flower petals into the bath as well as some teas. Fruity teas should be avoided because sugar can cause yeast infections, but chamomile is a relaxing, safe option. Rose petals in the bath will encourage love and romance. Lavender promotes calmness and peace of mind.

The faucet of the bath can represent flushing new, pure vibrations into your life. The drain of the bath is also symbolic. It can either represent flushing out negative energy, or represent sending your intentions out into the world.

You can enhance the ritual by playing music that compliments your intentions, lighting candles, and by keeping crystals nearby. Many crystals will degrade if immersed in water, so this is not recommended.

Conclusion

Whether or not you choose to observe the year and a day guideline, it is wise to have a period dedicated to learning the craft before you begin your practice. This protects you and those around you from potential unintended effects of inexperienced magick. Only you know when you are truly ready to begin. Trust your instincts, but remember that it's not a race! Everything will come to you in your own time.

Chapter 6: Finding Your Niche

With all this new information, it's easy to become overwhelmed. But choosing your path in Wicca is all about what traditions, rituals, and practices you connect with the most. Your craft doesn't have to be like anyone else's, it can and in many ways should be completely unique to your spiritual needs and beliefs.

Some traditional Wiccans believe in the concept of "a year and a day". This is the idea that a beginning witch should devote a year and one day to only learning and studying the Craft. This is most common within covens that have an initiation process once this time period has passed. If you want to practice with a group, this learning period also gives you time to learn about and bond with the other Wiccans in your coven. It also provides time for a beginner to familiarize themselves with the rules and traditions of the group.

Some solitary witches value this tradition and follow it, but many Wiccans don't believe in an exact set period of time. Of course it is encouraged to learn about and understand the Craft before you practice, lest you make a mistake and cause yourself or someone else harm by accident. The learning period, however long it may be for you, is also a sign of respect for the Craft. It shows that you know Wicca is not a fad or a phase, but something to be taken seriously.

Choosing Your Path

Outside of the major traditions, there are still many different acknowledged "types" of witches. Most witches fall into more than one category. By learning about each path, you can start to see what might interest you, and do further research on that subject to begin to specialize your knowledge. Don't be afraid to change your mind, and don't be afraid to experiment, as long as you do no harm.

Eclectic witches are Wiccans who combine many different beliefs, ideas, and traditions into their practice. An eclectic witch may worship multiple pantheons. Eclectic witches value practices from all cultures. They may practice divination from different areas of the world. Eclectic witches are almost always solitary, meaning they don't work with a group though they may participate in community gatherings for festivals.

Green witches, also known as garden witches or forest witches, are attracted to all things green. Green witches practice most of their magick outdoors. Many keep personal gardens, or grow houseplants if a garden is not available to them. They have a deep love for plants, flowers, herbs, and trees. Green witches are able to sense and connect with the spirits of plants, and prefer to use home-grown items for their Craft. Some even make offerings to their plants, or place crystals in the soil if the plant is potted.

Green witches are herbalists who have a wide range of knowledge about their local flora. They can identify plants by sight. They also gain a large range of knowledge about medicinal and poisonous plants through their diligent, passionate studies.

A *hedge witch* is a Wiccan who is skilled with spirit work. These individuals cross the metaphorical hedge to the other side for answers and guidance. Hedge witch is the modern word for a shaman. Many witches prefer to avoid identifying as shamans unless they descend from a shamanistic culture, because it can be appropriative and disrespectful to claim another culture's title.

Hedge witches communicate with spirits in a variety of ways. This is called hedgecrossing, no matter what method is used. Some meet and speak with spirits through lucid dreams. Lucid dreaming often comes naturally to a hedge witch, but it is a skill most can learn. Astral projection and trances are other ways to communicate with the spirit world.

Kitchen witches reject a lot of traditional perspectives, and strongly believe in finding magick in the mundane. These individuals thrive while cooking, making teas, brews, and working with herb and spice blends to enchant meals and drinks. If these tasks need to be performed either way, why not make them magickal?

Kitchen witches imbue their cooking with medicinal and magickal properties. For example, one might season food with rosemary to provide protection for the family and friends who will consume the food. Kitchen witches often have collections of recipes passed down from many generations.

An *augury witch* is a Wiccan who is able to interpret natural omens. Augury is an ancient Roman tradition. Augury witches often work with travelers to help guide them along the correct path. Augurs may interpret weather patterns or the appearance of sacred animals such as birds.

Hereditary witches are those who have other witches in the family. Some hereditary witches come from a long line of Wiccans. Others may find out they have a connection to Wicca by learning of an ancestor who practiced, as well as forming an interest in reclaiming the Craft.

You do not have to choose any label for your practice. Labels are meaningful and helpful to some, but can be confining and smothering for others. Some witches feel connected to the stars, some to fire, some to the ocean and some to the mountains. Commune with nature and the answers will come from within you.

COMMUNITY OUTREACH

Whether you're a solo witch or part of a coven, community is an important part of Wicca. Beginner witches are often affectionately known as "baby witches" and are cherished by the Wiccan community. Every Wiccan remembers the beginning of their journey and the kindness they received from others following the Old Religion. You will find they are eager to pay it forward by offering tips, friendship, and sometimes even mentorship.

Only about 1% of the world practices Wicca, which can make it challenging to find others in your area. Another obstacle is the stigma that still surrounds Wiccan beliefs. Many people don't understand the difference between white and black magick. They fear Wiccans as devil-worshippers who summon demons to do their bidding. However, as you know by this point, that couldn't be farther from the truth. Regardless, many Wiccans remain silent about their beliefs to avoid judgment from their friends, families, and communities.

The best way to connect with other Wiccans is online. Try searching social media tags for groups dedicated to the Craft. Be wary of those who would take advantage of you, and take the same precautions you normally would when communicating with strangers on the internet.

Luckily, the vast majority of the Wiccan community is warm and welcoming. Reaching out to other Wiccans is one of the best ways to find reliable information about the Old Religion. They can provide book recommendations written by qualified occult authors that provide legitimate information. When searching for information about Wicca on the internet, keep your wits about you; there is no shortage of phonies publishing misleading and incorrect information.

Conclusion

If you haven't realized it by now, Wicca can be full of contradictions. While this might be confusing for beginners, it is part of the beauty of the religion. As you continue to read and learn about Wicca, you will continue to encounter these contradictions. Your favorite authors might have different methods of casting a circle, or you may hear fellow Wiccans disputing the origins of certain traditions. When you come to these crossroads, it is time to tune into your intuition and make whatever decision makes most sense for you.

But you don't have to make these decisions all at once. In fact, it's always better to wait until you have adequate information before choosing any path. Research really is the name of the game when it comes to understanding ancient practices.

There is room for everyone who feels called to the Craft, and that means there is room for you, too!

www.ingramcontent.com/pod-product-compliance
Lightning Source LLC
Chambersburg PA
CBHW070047230426
43661CB00005B/799